McGRAW-HILL READING

Spelling

Grade 6 Practice Book

D1523497

McGraw-Hill
School Division

New York   Farmington

CONTENTS

Grade 6/Unit 1

Grade 6/Unit 2

Grade 6/Unit 3

Mummies, Tombs, & Treasure: Secrets of Ancient Egypt
Words with /sh/, /ch/, and /zh/

Over the Top of the World
Words with /ər/, /əl/, and /ən/

The Phantom Tollbooth
Spelling Unstressed Syllables

Exploring the Titanic
Words with Silent Letters

Back to the Moon!
Words from Science

Grade 6/Unit 5

Grade 6/Unit 6

Words with Short Vowels

Pretest Directions

Fold back the paper along the dotted line. Use the blanks to write each word as it is read aloud. When you finish the test, unfold the paper. Use the list at the right to correct any spelling mistakes. Practice the words you missed for the Posttest.

To Parents

Here are the results of your child's weekly spelling Pretest. You can help your child study for the Posttest by following these simple steps for each word on the word list:

1. Read the word to your child.

2. Have your child write the word, saying each letter as it is written.

3. Say each letter of the word as your child checks the spelling.

4. If a mistake has been made, have your child read each letter of the correctly spelled word aloud, and then repeat steps 1–3.

1. _____	1. pressure
2. _____	2. crafty
3. _____	3. prison
4. _____	4. cleanse
5. _____	5. rotten
6. _____	6. flung
7. _____	7. spongy
8. _____	8. tension
9. _____	9. abstract
10. _____	10. brilliant
11. _____	11. realm
12. _____	12. soccer
13. _____	13. plunge
14. _____	14. hover
15. _____	15. nectar
16. _____	16. badger
17. _____	17. missile
18. _____	18. novel
19. _____	19. summon
20. _____	20. singular

Challenge Words

_____ attitude

_____ bribe

_____ cringing

_____ defect

_____ treason

Words with Short Vowels

Using the Word Study Steps

1. LOOK at the word.
2. SAY the word aloud.
3. STUDY the letters in the word.
4. WRITE the word.
5. CHECK the word.

   Did you spell the word right?
   If not, go back to step 1.

Spelling Tip

Make up clues to help you remember the spelling.

You must be <u>craft</u>y to make a <u>raft</u>.

What is the <u>sum</u> of <u>sum</u>mon?

To h<u>over</u>, look <u>over</u>.

Word Scramble

Unscramble each set of letters to make a spelling word.

1. sccreo _____
2. glenup _____
3. tentro _____
4. eelscan _____
5. arguslin _____
6. vlone _____
7. ytfarc _____
8. rentac _____
9. pygons _____
10. slimeis _____

11. attsbrac _____
12. ropins _____
13. seesprur _____
14. mosumn _____
15. rhvoe _____
16. emral _____
17. lairblint _____
18. ngulf _____
19. dagbre _____
20. ennitos _____

To Parents or Helpers:

Using the Word Study Steps above as your child comes across any new words will help him or her learn to spell words effectively. Review the steps as you both go over this week's spelling words.

Go over the Spelling Tip with your child. Help your child make up a clue to help remember the spelling of one or more of the spelling words.

Help your child complete the word scramble.

Words with Short Vowels

pressure	rotten	abstract	plunge	missile
crafty	flung	brilliant	hover	novel
prison	spongy	realm	nectar	summon
cleanse	tension	soccer	badger	singular

Find the sound and spelling pattern in each spelling word's first syllable. Write the word and underline the letter that spells its vowel sound.

Short /a/ spelled

a

1. _____

2. _____

3. _____

Short /o/ spelled

o

4. _____

5. _____

6. _____

Short /u/ spelled

u

7. _____

8. _____

9. _____

o

10. _____

11. _____

Short /e/ spelled

e

12. _____

13. _____

14. _____

ea

15. _____

16. _____

Short /i/ spelled

i

17. _____

18. _____

19. _____

20. _____

Words with Short Vowels

pressure	rotten	abstract	plunge	missile
crafty	flung	brilliant	hover	novel
prison	spongy	realm	nectar	summon
cleanse	tension	soccer	badger	singular

Analogies

An **analogy** is a statement that compares the relationship between pairs of words. Use spelling words to complete the analogies below.

1. *Castle* is to *palace* as *jail* is to _____.

2. *Open* is to *closed* as *concrete* is to _____.

3. *Flower* is to *daffodil* as *weapon* is to _____.

4. *Upward* is to *leap* as *downward* is to _____.

5. *Go* is to *dismiss* as *come* is to _____.

6. *Home run* is to *baseball* as *goal* is to _____.

7. *Angry* is to *furious* as *kingdom* is to _____.

8. *Stanza* is to *poem* as *chapter* is to _____.

What Does It Mean?

Fill in the spelling word that best matches each definition.

9. spoiled _____

10. sweet liquid _____

11. only _____

12. force _____

13. wash _____

14. small animal _____

15. very smart _____

16. absorbent _____

17. clever _____

18. hurled _____

19. nervousness _____

20. linger over _____

Challenge Extension: Draw one picture which includes an illustration of all five Challenge Words. Trade pictures with a partner. Find and label the Challenge Words on each other's picture.

Words with Short Vowels

Proofreading Activity

There are six spelling mistakes in the paragraph below. Circle the misspelled words. Write the words correctly on the lines below.

The preshir was on! If we failed to win the last baseball game of the year, it would plunj us into despair. We would lose our honor as briliant players who weren't the biggest or strongest, but could always win by thinking faster than the other team. Tenshun filled our dugout at the bottom of the ninth inning. Our team was down by one point. Katie, our pitcher, flunge the ball toward the batter. CRACK! The long fly ball seemed to hovir in the air as it headed to the outfield. Suddenly, I jumped high in the air and caught it on the tip of my glove. I'd saved the game for our team!

1. _____   3. _____   5. _____

2. _____   4. _____   6. _____

Writing Activity

What was the most exciting moment you ever watched or experienced in a sporting contest? Write a sports article about what happened. Use four spelling words in your writing.

_____

_____

_____

_____

Words with Short Vowels

Look at the words in each set below. One word in each set is spelled correctly. Use a pencil to fill in the circle next to the correct word. Before you begin, look at the sample sets of words. Sample A has been done for you. Do Sample B by yourself. When you are sure you know what to do, you may go on with the rest of the page.

Sample A:
- (A) truk
- (B) truhk
- ● truck
- (D) truhck

Sample B:
- (E) curtain
- (F) kertin
- (G) curtin
- (H) curtan

1.
- (A) plunge
- (B) plunj
- (C) plundge
- (D) plunch

2.
- (E) necktar
- (F) nectir
- (G) nectar
- (H) necter

3.
- (A) craffty
- (B) crafty
- (C) craftie
- (D) crifty

4.
- (E) ebstract
- (F) abstrect
- (G) abstract
- (H) abstrackt

5.
- (A) novil
- (B) novel
- (C) noval
- (D) novell

6.
- (E) flung
- (F) flungg
- (G) flong
- (H) flongg

7.
- (A) sengular
- (B) singuler
- (C) singullar
- (D) singular

8.
- (E) prizon
- (F) prison
- (G) prizzon
- (H) prisin

9.
- (A) bager
- (B) bajer
- (C) badgir
- (D) badger

10.
- (E) cleanse
- (F) clenns
- (G) cleanns
- (H) cleanz

11.
- (A) soccer
- (B) socker
- (C) soccir
- (D) sockir

12.
- (E) brilliant
- (F) brillian
- (G) brillant
- (H) brilant

13.
- (A) missil
- (B) missill
- (C) missile
- (D) misille

14.
- (E) sumonn
- (F) summon
- (G) sumon
- (H) summun

15.
- (A) tenshun
- (B) tenzion
- (C) tention
- (D) tension

16.
- (E) pressure
- (F) prassure
- (G) preshure
- (H) pressire

17.
- (A) sponjy
- (B) spongy
- (C) spongie
- (D) spungy

18.
- (E) rottin
- (F) rotten
- (G) rottan
- (H) rottun

19.
- (A) rellm
- (B) reallm
- (C) realmn
- (D) realm

20.
- (E) hovir
- (F) hover
- (G) hovar
- (H) huver

Words with Long *a* and Long *e*

Pretest Directions

Fold back the paper along the dotted line. Use the blanks to write each word as it is read aloud. When you finish the test, unfold the paper. Use the list at the right to correct any spelling mistakes. Practice the words you missed for the Posttest.

To Parents

Here are the results of your child's weekly spelling Pretest. You can help your child study for the Posttest by following these simple steps for each word on the word list:

1. Read the word to your child.

2. Have your child write the word, saying each letter as it is written.

3. Say each letter of the word as your child checks the spelling.

4. If a mistake has been made, have your child read each letter of the correctly spelled word aloud, and then repeat steps 1–3.

1. _____	1. bathe
2. _____	2. exclaimed
3. _____	3. complete
4. _____	4. relief
5. _____	5. debate
6. _____	6. navy
7. _____	7. cheat
8. _____	8. keen
9. _____	9. retreat
10. _____	10. grief
11. _____	11. pave
12. _____	12. obtain
13. _____	13. basin
14. _____	14. grease
15. _____	15. scheme
16. _____	16. niece
17. _____	17. canteen
18. _____	18. disgraced
19. _____	19. supreme
20. _____	20. trait

Challenge Words

_____ acquainted

_____ buffet

_____ inflections

_____ residence

_____ rummage

Words with Long *a* and Long *e*

Using the Word Study Steps

1. LOOK at the word.
2. SAY the word aloud.
3. STUDY the letters in the word.
4. WRITE the word.
5. CHECK the word.

   Did you spell the word right?
   If not, go back to step 1.

Spelling Tip

To choose between *ei* or *ie*, remember this rhyme:
   i before *e*,
   except after *c*
   or when sounded
      like *a*
   as in *neighbor*
      or *weigh*.
gr<u>ie</u>f n<u>ie</u>ce rec<u>ei</u>ve sl<u>ei</u>gh

Alphabetical Order

Write the spelling words in alphabetical order.

1. _____
2. _____
3. _____
4. _____
5. _____
6. _____
7. _____
8. _____
9. _____
10. _____

11. _____
12. _____
13. _____
14. _____
15. _____
16. _____
17. _____
18. _____
19. _____
20. _____

To Parents or Helpers:

   Using the Word Study Steps above as your child comes across any new words will help him or her learn to spell words effectively. Review the steps as you both go over this week's spelling words.

   Go over the Spelling Tip with your child. Ask your child if he or she can think of other words that follow the *ie* and *ei* rule.

   Help your child complete the spelling activity.

Words with Long *a* and Long *e*

bathe	debate	retreat	basin	canteen
exclaimed	navy	grief	grease	disgraced
complete	cheat	pave	scheme	supreme
relief	keen	obtain	niece	trait

Write the spelling words with each of the spelling patterns below.

Long *a* spelled

a-e

1. _____

2. _____

3. _____

4. _____

ai

5. _____

6. _____

7. _____

a

8. _____

9. _____

Long *e* spelled

ea

10. _____

11. _____

12. _____

ee

13. _____

14. _____

e-e

15. _____

16. _____

17. _____

ie

18. _____

19. _____

20. _____

Guide Words

Guide words at the top of each page in a dictionary show the first and last words on that page. Write which spelling word would be on the page that had the following guide words:

21. oats/often _____

23. dare/decide _____

22. ball/bat _____

24. traffic/trunk _____

Words with Long *a* and Long *e*

bathe	debate	retreat	basin	canteen
exclaimed	navy	grief	grease	disgraced
complete	cheat	pave	scheme	supreme
relief	keen	obtain	niece	trait

Antonyms

An **antonym** is a word that means the opposite of another word. Find the spelling word that is an antonym for each word below.

1. undone _____

2. worst _____

3. advance _____

4. dull _____

5. unsaid _____

6. agree _____

7. lose _____

8. honored _____

9. stress _____

10. joy _____

Complete the Sentence

Write the spelling word that best completes each sentence.

11. It feels good to _____ in warm water on a cold day.

12. I had _____ on my hands after changing the tire.

13. My cousin Mary is my mother's _____.

14. Honesty is a character _____, like kindness or courage.

15. The _____ is a fast place to go for a bite to eat.

16. We must find someone to _____ the school's driveway.

17. I don't _____ because it makes me feel ashamed.

18. They thought up a _____ to make money selling old buttons.

19. A soldier belongs to the army and a sailor belongs to the _____.

20. They carried a _____ of water outside to give the dog a bath.

Challenge Extension: Write a short story about something funny that might happen in a restaurant. Use all five Challenge Words in your writing.

Grade 6/Unit 1
The All-American Slurp

20

Words with Long *a* and Long *e*

Proofreading Activity
There are six spelling mistakes in the paragraph below. Circle the misspelled words. Write the words correctly on the lines below.

My best friend Grina and I came up with a scheem to get together. I would visit her in her Caribbean home of Dominica for two weeks in August. After a long deebate with my parents, they agreed I could go if I worked to obtane the money to pay for my plane ticket. All through June and July I made the suprime sacrifice of working in a grocery store while my friends had fun at the beach. What a releaf it was when I finally had enough money to buy my ticket! Since my part of the bargain was complet, I could now look forward to a lazy, sunny vacation with my friend.

1. _____   3. _____   5. _____

2. _____   4. _____   6. _____

Writing Activity
What country would you like to visit? Pretend that you are visiting that country. Write a letter to a friend back home telling what experiences you are having. Use four spelling words in your writing.

_____

_____

_____

_____

Words with Long *a* and Long *e*

Look at the words in each set below. One word in each set is spelled correctly. Use a pencil to fill in the circle next to the correct word. Before you begin, look at the sample sets of words. Sample A has been done for you. Do Sample B by yourself. When you are sure you know what to do, you may go on with the rest of the page.

Sample A:
- (A) bleak
- (B) bleek
- (C) bleack
- (D) bleeck

Sample B:
- (E) saiv
- (F) saev
- (G) save
- (H) sayv

1.
- (A) disgrased
- (B) disgrasd
- (C) disgraced
- (D) disgracd

2.
- (E) cheet
- (F) cheat
- (G) chete
- (H) cheate

3.
- (A) exclaimed
- (B) exclamed
- (C) exclamd
- (D) exclaimd

4.
- (E) supreme
- (F) sapreme
- (G) supreime
- (H) saprieme

5.
- (A) paiv
- (B) paive
- (C) pave
- (D) pav

6.
- (E) ritreat
- (F) retreat
- (G) ritreet
- (H) retreet

7.
- (A) bathe
- (B) baith
- (C) baeth
- (D) baethe

8.
- (E) griece
- (F) grease
- (G) grese
- (H) greese

9.
- (A) scheme
- (B) sckeme
- (C) scheem
- (D) sckeem

10.
- (E) cantene
- (F) canteene
- (G) cantein
- (H) canteen

11.
- (A) abtain
- (B) obtane
- (C) obtain
- (D) abtane

12.
- (E) cumplete
- (F) compleet
- (G) complete
- (H) compleete

13.
- (A) rilief
- (B) ralief
- (C) releif
- (D) relief

14.
- (E) keen
- (F) kien
- (G) kein
- (H) keene

15.
- (A) basen
- (B) basan
- (C) basin
- (D) basun

16.
- (E) trate
- (F) traet
- (G) trait
- (H) trat

17.
- (A) navy
- (B) navie
- (C) navee
- (D) nayvy

18.
- (E) dabate
- (F) debate
- (G) dibate
- (H) debat

19.
- (A) neice
- (B) neece
- (C) neese
- (D) niece

20.
- (E) greef
- (F) grefe
- (G) greif
- (H) grief

Words with Long *i* and Long *o*

Pretest Directions

Fold back the paper along the dotted line. Use the blanks to write each word as it is read aloud. When you finish the test, unfold the paper. Use the list at the right to correct any spelling mistakes. Practice the words you missed for the Posttest.

To Parents

Here are the results of your child's weekly spelling Pretest. You can help your child study for the Posttest by following these simple steps for each word on the word list:

1. Read the word to your child.

2. Have your child write the word, saying each letter as it is written.

3. Say each letter of the word as your child checks the spelling.

4. If a mistake has been made, have your child read each letter of the correctly spelled word aloud, and then repeat steps 1–3.

1. _____	1. spine
2. _____	2. omit
3. _____	3. reminded
4. _____	4. deny
5. _____	5. soak
6. _____	6. private
7. _____	7. poet
8. _____	8. boast
9. _____	9. doe
10. _____	10. tying
11. _____	11. devote
12. _____	12. rhyme
13. _____	13. likewise
14. _____	14. quote
15. _____	15. foe
16. _____	16. skyline
17. _____	17. minor
18. _____	18. strive
19. _____	19. bonus
20. _____	20. oboe

Challenge Words

_____	destination
_____	majestic
_____	mongrel
_____	protruding
_____	silhouetted

Name_____ Date_____ **Spelling**

Words with Long *i* and Long *o*

Using the Word Study Steps

1. LOOK at the word
2. SAY the word aloud.
3. STUDY the letters in the word.
4. WRITE the word.
5. CHECK the word.

   Did you spell the word right?
   If not, go back to step 1.

Spelling Tip

Words you know how to spell can help you spell new words.

queen   <u>n</u>ote = <u>quote</u>

spring   <u>l</u>ine = <u>spine</u>

Cross out the Word

Put an X on the one word that does *not* rhyme with the spelling word on the left.

1. **boast**	coast	boat	toast
2. **likewise**	surprise	retries	freeze
3. **minor**	liner	shiner	door
4. **tying**	frying	skiing	sighing
5. **devote**	promote	denote	divide
6. **foe**	two	show	no
7. **rhyme**	chime	slim	time
8. **soak**	choke	stoke	stock
9. **deny**	sigh	reply	life
10. **omit**	write	quit	sit

To Parents or Helpers:

Using the Word Study Steps above as your child comes across any new words will help him or her learn to spell words effectively. Review the steps as you both go over this week's spelling words.

Go over the Spelling Tip with your child. Ask your child to pick a spelling word that is new. See if your child can think of words he or she already knows that could help him or her remember how to spell the new word.

Help your child complete the spelling activity.

Grade 6/Unit 1
Viva New Jersey

Words with Long *i* and Long *o*

spine	soak	doe	likewise	minor
omit	private	tying	quote	strive
reminded	poet	devote	foe	bonus
deny	boast	rhyme	skyline	oboe

Write the spelling words with each of these spelling patterns.

Long *i* spelled

i-e

1. _____
2. _____
3. _____

i

4. _____
5. _____
6. _____

y

7. _____
8. _____
9. _____
10. _____

Long *o* spelled

o-e

11. _____
12. _____

oa

13. _____
14. _____

o

15. _____
16. _____
17. _____

oe

18. _____
19. _____
20. _____

Mark the Word

Put a "1" next to the spelling words that have one syllable. Put a "2" next to the spelling words that have two syllables.

21. omit _____

22. deny _____

23. private _____

24. soak _____

25. rhyme _____

26. boast _____

Words with Long *i* and Long *o*

spine	soak	doe	likewise	minor
omit	private	tying	quote	strive
reminded	poet	devote	foe	bonus
deny	boast	rhyme	skyline	oboe

Word Meanings: Antonyms

Write the spelling word that is the opposite of each word below.

1. include _____

2. major _____

3. friend _____

4. public _____

5. admit _____

6. dry _____

Write the spelling word that best matches each definition.

7. writer _____

8. backbone _____

9. brag _____

10. same sound _____

11. female deer _____

12. told again _____

Complete each sentence below with a spelling word or words.

13. The _____ shows the shapes of buildings against the sky.

14. To have a good friend, you must _____ to be a good friend.

15. He got two _____ points for answering that question so well.

16. The _____ is from the woodwind family, just like the flute.

17. Did the newspaper _____ the president's speech?

18. Watch how he draws the face and then do _____.

19. The volunteers _____ most of their time to helping the elderly.

20. The 5-year-old girl has started _____ her own shoes.

Challenge Extension: Have students look up each Challenge Word in the dictionary. Then ask them to make up one fill-in sentence for each word. Have partners exchange papers, filling in each other's sentences with the correct Challenge Word.

Words with Long *i* and Long *o*

Proofreading Activity

There are six spelling mistakes in this paragraph. Circle the misspelled words. Write the words correctly on the lines below.

   Tamara looked out her bedroom window at the skilyne of Philadelphia. She was not daydreaming, she was worried. She could not denie it; something terrible had happened. While she was out, her cat Hyde had vanished from the apartment. She had looked everywhere. He was not sleeping in his privat corner in the closet. He was not tucked tightly into her open oboh case. Likwise, he was not snoozing on top of the piano. While Tamara was searching the living room, she felt a slight breeze on her face. That riminded her that the living room window was half open. She rushed over and there was Hyde, lying on the fire escape.

1. _____   3. _____   5. _____

2. _____   4. _____   6. _____

Writing Activity

What would you do if you couldn't find your pet? Write a story about looking for a pet. Use four spelling words in your writing.

_____

_____

_____

_____

Words with Long *i* and Long *o*

Look at the words in each set below. One word in each set is spelled correctly. Use a pencil to fill in the circle next to the correct word. Before you begin, look at the sample sets of words. Sample A has been done for you. Do Sample B by yourself. When you are sure you know what to do, you may go on with the rest of the page.

Sample A:
- (A) stofe
- (B) stov
- (C) stoov
- (D) stove ●

Sample B:
- (E) bote
- (F) bot
- (G) boat
- (H) baot

1.
- (A) obo
- (B) oboe
- (C) ohbo
- (D) obow

2.
- (E) spein
- (F) spine
- (G) spyn
- (H) spyne

3.
- (A) private
- (B) privite
- (C) privut
- (D) privute

4.
- (E) ryme
- (F) reim
- (G) rhym
- (H) rhyme

5.
- (A) strive
- (B) streive
- (C) striev
- (D) striv

6.
- (E) boste
- (F) boast
- (G) boaste
- (H) bost

7.
- (A) deny
- (B) denie
- (C) diny
- (D) dinie

8.
- (E) skiline
- (F) skieline
- (G) skyline
- (H) skylin

9.
- (A) fo
- (B) fou
- (C) fow
- (D) foe

10.
- (E) minor
- (F) minur
- (G) mynor
- (H) mynir

11.
- (A) riminded
- (B) reminded
- (C) raminded
- (D) remineded

12.
- (E) likewize
- (F) likwize
- (G) likewise
- (H) likwise

13.
- (A) dow
- (B) doe
- (C) dou
- (D) doh

14.
- (E) tying
- (F) tieing
- (G) tyng
- (H) ting

15.
- (A) davote
- (B) devot
- (C) davot
- (D) devote

16.
- (E) soke
- (F) sok
- (G) soek
- (H) soak

17.
- (A) ohmit
- (B) omit
- (C) umit
- (D) omitt

18.
- (E) quot
- (F) qote
- (G) quote
- (H) qot

19.
- (A) bonis
- (B) bonus
- (C) bonice
- (D) bonuss

20.
- (E) poet
- (F) powit
- (G) poette
- (H) powette

Words with /ū/ and /ü/

Pretest Directions

Fold back the paper along the dotted line. Use the blanks to write each word as it is read aloud. When you finish the test, unfold the paper. Use the list at the right to correct any spelling mistakes. Practice the words you missed for the Posttest.

To Parents

Here are the results of your child's weekly spelling Pretest. You can help your child study for the Posttest by following these simple steps for each word on the word list:

1. Read the word to your child.

2. Have your child write the word, saying each letter as it is written.

3. Say each letter of the word as your child checks the spelling.

4. If a mistake has been made, have your child read each letter of the correctly spelled word aloud, and then repeat steps 1–3.

#		#	Word
1.	_____	1.	value
2.	_____	2.	proof
3.	_____	3.	rude
4.	_____	4.	usually
5.	_____	5.	issue
6.	_____	6.	funeral
7.	_____	7.	mute
8.	_____	8.	sinew
9.	_____	9.	shrewd
10.	_____	10.	solution
11.	_____	11.	troop
12.	_____	12.	absolute
13.	_____	13.	cue
14.	_____	14.	pursue
15.	_____	15.	universe
16.	_____	16.	perfume
17.	_____	17.	groove
18.	_____	18.	casually
19.	_____	19.	curfew
20.	_____	20.	sewer

Challenge Words

_____ existence

_____ jubilantly

_____ pedestals

_____ psychology

_____ subdued

Words with /ū/ and /ü/

Using the Word Study Steps

1. LOOK at the word.
2. SAY the word aloud.
3. STUDY the letters in the word.
4. WRITE the word.
5. CHECK the word.

   Did you spell the word right?
   If not, go back to step 1.

Spelling Tip

Look for word chunks or smaller words that help you remember the spelling of the word.

curfew = cur few
absolute = ab so lute

Where are the spelling words?

Find and circle the spelling words in the puzzle below.

```
c s i n e w m a b s o l u t e w s o l u t i o n
f u n e r a l x i s s u e c p u r s u e r u d e
r s u n i v e r s e u o g r o o v e v m u t e e
n p r o o f c d c u e h k s h r e w d t r o o p
w p e r f u m e w v a l u e b v u s u a l l y v
x f c u r f e w c a s u a l l y w x s e w e r v
```

To Parents or Helpers:

Using the Word Study Steps above as your child comes across any new words will help him or her learn to spell words effectively. Review the steps as you both go over this week's spelling words.

Go over the Spelling Tip with your child. Ask him or her to find other spelling words containing word chunks or smaller words.

Help your child find the spelling words in the puzzle.

Name_____ Date_____

Words with /ū/ and /ü/

value	issue	shrewd	cue	groove
proof	funeral	solution	pursue	casually
rude	mute	troop	universe	curfew
usually	sinew	absolute	perfume	sewer

Write the spelling words for each spelling pattern below.

Long /ū/ spelled: **Long /ü/ spelled:**

u-e   *u-e*

1. _____   10. _____

2. _____   11. _____

u   *u*

3. _____   12. _____

4. _____   13. _____

5. _____   14. _____

ew   *oo*

6. _____   15. _____

7. _____   16. _____

ue   17. _____

8. _____   *ew*

9. _____   18. _____

                          19. _____

                          ue

                          20. _____

                          21. _____

The Two *U*'s

Which spelling word has both the /ū/ and /ü/ sounds? Write the spelling word and underline the letter spelling each of the two vowel sounds.

22. _____

Words with /ū/ and /ü/

value	issue	shrewd	cue	groove
proof	funeral	solution	pursue	casually
rude	mute	troop	universe	curfew
usually	sinew	absolute	perfume	sewer

Word Meaning: Synonyms

Write the spelling word that has the same meaning as the words below.

1. silent _____

2. worth _____

3. impolite _____

4. scent _____

5. muscle _____

6. follow _____

7. complete _____

8. clever _____

9. signal _____

10. mostly _____

Complete each sentence below with a spelling word.

11. Do you have the first _____ of the school newsletter?

12. He _____ strolled across the street, without a care.

13. This circus has a _____ of six or eight acrobats.

14. President Kennedy's _____ saddened the nation.

15. A math problem has only one correct _____.

16. The detective had _____ that the person was a thief.

17. There are many other planets besides Earth in the _____.

18. A plumber was called to check on the school's _____ system.

19. The front wheel of my bike made a _____ in the sand.

20. My _____ on school nights is 7 P.M.

Challenge Extension: Write a definition for each of the
Challenge Words. Then exchange papers with partners
and write the spelling words beside each definition.

Words with /ū/ and /ü/

Proofreading Activity

There are six spelling mistakes in the story below. Circle the misspelled words. Write the words correctly on the lines below.

Tom leaned out of the window to look at the sky. "I promise that it won't rain today," he stated. Karen looked doubtful. "Your promise is not prouf that it won't rain. I'm taking my umbrella, just in case." Tom pretended to be insulted. "It's roode not to believe me," he joked. Anyway, it wouldn't dare rain before my curfue at nine o'clock." Karen and Tom went to the ballgame. The ball field was freshly mowed and had the perfoom of cut grass. Their star player, Luke, stepped up to the plate. Tom and Karen could see the senews of his arms as he gripped the bat. Then he swung hard. Everyone watched the ball pursew its course high out of the park. It was a grand slam!

1. _____   3. _____   5. _____

2. _____   4. _____   6. _____

Writing Activity

Write a conversation you and a friend might have about getting caught in the rain at a ballgame. Use four spelling words in your writing.

_____

_____

_____

_____

Words with /ū/ and /ü/

Look at the words in each set below. One word in each set is spelled correctly. Use a pencil to fill in the circle next to the correct word. Before you begin, look at the sample sets of words. Sample A has been done for you. Do Sample B by yourself. When you are sure you know what to do, you may go on with the rest of the page.

Sample A:
- Ⓐ troo
- Ⓑ tru
- Ⓒ true
- Ⓓ troe

Sample B:
- Ⓔ baloon
- Ⓕ balloon
- Ⓖ baluen
- Ⓗ balluen

1. Ⓐ sewer
   Ⓑ sooer
   Ⓒ soor
   Ⓓ sewir

2. Ⓔ pursoo
   Ⓕ pursue
   Ⓖ pursew
   Ⓗ pirsue

3. Ⓐ myute
   Ⓑ miute
   Ⓒ mewt
   Ⓓ mute

4. Ⓔ shrewd
   Ⓕ shrood
   Ⓖ shreud
   Ⓗ shreiud

5. Ⓐ troop
   Ⓑ trop
   Ⓒ trupe
   Ⓓ trewp

6. Ⓔ fewneril
   Ⓕ funeral
   Ⓖ funeril
   Ⓗ fewneral

7. Ⓐ yuniverse
   Ⓑ yooniverse
   Ⓒ univirse
   Ⓓ universe

8. Ⓔ perfewm
   Ⓕ pirfume
   Ⓖ perfume
   Ⓗ parfume

9. Ⓐ rude
   Ⓑ ruhd
   Ⓒ rewd
   Ⓓ ruud

10. Ⓔ prof
    Ⓕ prouf
    Ⓖ proof
    Ⓗ prewf

11. Ⓐ senew
    Ⓑ sinew
    Ⓒ sinyou
    Ⓓ sinue

12. Ⓔ kue
    Ⓕ ciu
    Ⓖ cue
    Ⓗ ciew

13. Ⓐ absalute
    Ⓑ absaloot
    Ⓒ absolut
    Ⓓ absolute

14. Ⓔ velue
    Ⓕ value
    Ⓖ valu
    Ⓗ velew

15. Ⓐ isue
    Ⓑ issue
    Ⓒ izue
    Ⓓ issew

16. Ⓔ solution
    Ⓕ salution
    Ⓖ solucion
    Ⓗ selution

17. Ⓐ greuve
    Ⓑ groov
    Ⓒ greuv
    Ⓓ groove

18. Ⓔ uzually
    Ⓕ usualy
    Ⓖ usally
    Ⓗ usually

19. Ⓐ casually
    Ⓑ cazually
    Ⓒ casualy
    Ⓓ cazualy

20. Ⓔ curfyou
    Ⓕ curfu
    Ⓖ curfew
    Ⓗ curfue

Words from Social Studies

Pretest Directions

Fold back the paper along the dotted line. Use the blanks to write each word as it is read aloud. When you finish the test, unfold the paper. Use the list at the right to correct any spelling mistakes. Practice the words you missed for the Posttest.

To Parents

Here are the results of your child's weekly spelling Pretest. You can help your child study for the Posttest by following these simple steps for each word on the word list:

1. Read the word to your child.

2. Have your child write the word, saying each letter as it is written.

3. Say each letter of the word as your child checks the spelling.

4. If a mistake has been made, have your child read each letter of the correctly spelled word aloud, and then repeat steps 1–3.

1. _____	1. western
2. _____	2. navigate
3. _____	3. lighthouse
4. _____	4. distant
5. _____	5. oars
6. _____	6. southern
7. _____	7. historical
8. _____	8. tropical
9. _____	9. peninsula
10. _____	10. parallel
11. _____	11. cargo
12. _____	12. isle
13. _____	13. passage
14. _____	14. eastern
15. _____	15. hemisphere
16. _____	16. foreign
17. _____	17. latitude
18. _____	18. longitude
19. _____	19. ashore
20. _____	20. global

Challenge Words

_____	dreamer
_____	landmarks
_____	precise
_____	rudder
_____	technology

Words from Social Studies

Using the Word Study Steps

1. LOOK at the word.
2. SAY the word aloud.
3. STUDY the letters in the word.
4. WRITE the word.
5. CHECK the word.

   Did you spell the word right?
   If not, go back to step 1.

Spelling Tip

In a notebook, keep an alphabetical Personal Word List. List words you often have trouble spelling.

Word Scramble

Unscramble each set of letters to make a spelling word.

1. orgac _____
2. egsaasp _____
3. tntasid _____
4. etivagan _____
5. duetiglno _____
6. nrseetw _____
7. aplarlel _____
8. gnroeif _____
9. renhtous _____
10. aclioprt _____

11. ablolg _____
12. luasninep _____
13. lacitihros _____
14. saro _____
15. hpeersimhe _____
16. rntesae _____
17. esli _____
18. seuothhgil _____
19. reohsa _____
20. edtuiatl _____

To Parents or Helpers:

Using the Word Study Steps above as your child comes across any new words will help him or her learn to spell words effectively. Review the steps as you both go over this week's spelling words.

Go over the Spelling Tip with your child. Help your child create his or her own Personal Word List. If your child already has one, ask him or her if there are any new words he or she has trouble spelling that should be added to the list.

Help your child complete the word scramble.

Words from Social Studies

western	oars	peninsula	passage	latitude
navigate	southern	parallel	eastern	longitude
lighthouse	historical	cargo	hemisphere	ashore
distant	tropical	isle	foreign	global

Write the spelling words for each of the spelling patterns below.

One Syllable Words

1. _____
2. _____

Two Syllable Words

3. _____
4. _____
5. _____
6. _____
7. _____
8. _____
9. _____
10. _____
11. _____
12. _____

Three Syllable Words

13. _____
14. _____
15. _____
16. _____
17. _____
18. _____

Four Syllable Words

19. _____
20. _____

Words from Social Studies

western	oars	peninsula	passage	latitude
navigate	southern	parallel	eastern	longitude
lighthouse	historical	cargo	hemisphere	ashore
distant	tropical	isle	foreign	global

Write the spelling word that best matches the word or phrase below.

1. sphere half _____

2. on land _____

3. tower of light _____

4. small island _____

5. guide _____

6. worldwide _____

7. in the past _____

8. far away _____

Write the three spelling words that indicate compass direction.

9. _____   **10.** _____   **11.** _____

Write the spelling word that completes each sentence below.

12. She booked _____ on the ship and now has her ticket.

13. The ship carried its _____ of new cars to Europe.

14. Use the rowboat's _____ to keep it moving in a straight line.

15. Hot rain forests are found in _____ areas near the equator.

16. The lines will never meet because they are _____.

17. Drive down the _____ that juts into the ocean.

18. If he is not from this country, he is _____.

19. The lines of _____ run around the width of the globe.

20. The lines of _____ run north and south on the globe.

Challenge Extension: Use the dictionary to look up
each Challenge Word. Work with a partner taking turns
using each Challenge Word in a sentence.

Words from Social Studies

Proofreading Activity

There are six spelling mistakes in this story. Circle the misspelled words. Write the words correctly on the lines below.

Jim peered through the night fog at the distent light. "I see it!" he cried. "I see the litehouse!" Doc bent forward, pulling hard on both orz. They had been thrown overboard when their ship capsized, and both had clung to an overturned rowboat. They had righted the boat, salvaged some cargoe from the water, and headed in what they hoped was the direction of land. They had no clues to help them navvigate, only water as far as they could see. The light gave them fresh courage. They rowed toward land. Soon they would come ashor and be safe.

1. _____ 3. _____ 5. _____

2. _____ 4. _____ 6. _____

Writing Activity

Suppose you are sailing toward a great adventure. Where would you go? Write about your sailing adventure. Use four spelling words in your writing.

_____

_____

_____

_____

Words from Social Studies

Look at the words in each set below. One word in each set is spelled correctly. Use a pencil to fill in the circle next to the correct word. Before you begin, look at the sample sets of words. Sample A has been done for you. Do Sample B by yourself. When you are sure you know what to do, you may go on with the rest of the page.

Sample A:
- (A) stareboard
- (B) starbird
- (C) starboard
- (D) starrbird

Sample B:
- (E) ocean
- (F) oshun
- (G) ochen
- (H) oshean

1.
- (A) ashore
- (B) ashure
- (C) ashor
- (D) asshure

2.
- (E) troppical
- (F) tropiccal
- (G) tropical
- (H) tropicall

3.
- (A) passaje
- (B) passage
- (C) passadge
- (D) pasage

4.
- (E) parallel
- (F) parralel
- (G) paralell
- (H) parrallel

5.
- (A) oarz
- (B) oars
- (C) ors
- (D) orez

6.
- (E) peninnsula
- (F) penninsulla
- (G) peninsula
- (H) peninsoola

7.
- (A) isle
- (B) ile
- (C) ial
- (D) islle

8.
- (E) lattitude
- (F) latitud
- (G) lattitud
- (H) latitude

9.
- (A) cargoe
- (B) carrgo
- (C) carggo
- (D) cargo

10.
- (E) litehouse
- (F) lighthouse
- (G) lightouse
- (H) litehous

11.
- (A) hemsphere
- (B) hemisphere
- (C) hemmispher
- (D) hemispher

12.
- (E) wesstern
- (F) westirn
- (G) western
- (H) wesstirn

13.
- (A) historicall
- (B) historrical
- (C) historical
- (D) historricall

14.
- (E) distant
- (F) disstant
- (G) distent
- (H) disstent

15.
- (A) eestern
- (B) eastern
- (C) eastirn
- (D) eestirn

16.
- (E) forriegn
- (F) foreign
- (G) foriegn
- (H) forreign

17.
- (A) longitude
- (B) longitud
- (C) longetude
- (D) longetud

18.
- (E) global
- (F) globel
- (G) globell
- (H) globall

19.
- (A) navvigate
- (B) navigate
- (C) navigat
- (D) navvigat

20.
- (E) southern
- (F) suthern
- (G) southirn
- (H) southirne

Grade 6/Unit 1 Review Test

Read each sentence. If an underlined word is spelled wrong, fill in the circle that goes with that word. If no word is spelled wrong, fill in the circle below NONE.

Read Sample A and do Sample B.

NONE

A. The girl <u>explaned</u> that the <u>snow</u> was too <u>deep</u>.
          A   **B**   **C**
A. Ⓐ Ⓑ Ⓒ Ⓓ

NONE

B. She <u>decided</u> to <u>shovel</u> the drifts on the <u>stoop</u>.
      E   **F**   **G**
B. Ⓔ Ⓕ Ⓖ Ⓗ

NONE

1. My <u>briliant</u> <u>niece</u> plays the <u>oboe</u>.
     A   **B**   **C**
1. Ⓐ Ⓑ Ⓒ Ⓓ

NONE

2. He will <u>devote</u> his time to this <u>abstract</u> <u>scheme</u>.
        E   **F**   **G**
2. Ⓔ Ⓕ Ⓖ Ⓗ

NONE

3. The <u>litehouse</u> on the <u>peninsula</u> helped them <u>navigate</u>.
      A   **B**   **C**
3. Ⓐ Ⓑ Ⓒ Ⓓ

NONE

4. My <u>niece</u> will <u>bathe</u> with a <u>spongy</u> mitt.
      E   **F**   **G**
4. Ⓔ Ⓕ Ⓖ Ⓗ

NONE

5. The <u>novel</u> is hard to read and is, <u>likewize</u>, <u>abstract</u>.
      A   **B**   **C**
5. Ⓐ Ⓑ Ⓒ Ⓓ

NONE

6. The sailor's <u>funerul</u> is in the <u>lighthouse</u> on the <u>isle</u>.
         E   **F**   **G**
6. Ⓔ Ⓕ Ⓖ Ⓗ

NONE

7. "This <u>necter</u> has a <u>keen</u> taste," she <u>exclaimed</u>.
      A   **B**   **C**
7. Ⓐ Ⓑ Ⓒ Ⓓ

NONE

8. The <u>brilliant</u> boy <u>cazually</u> explained his <u>scheme</u>.
     E   **F**   **G**
8. Ⓔ Ⓕ Ⓖ Ⓗ

NONE

9. I can't <u>deny</u> that the land on this <u>peninsula</u> is <u>spongie</u>.
      A   **B**   **C**
9. Ⓐ Ⓑ Ⓒ Ⓓ

NONE

10. In <u>tropical</u> countries, a <u>cerfew</u> is <u>casually</u> followed.
      E   **F**   **G**
10. Ⓔ Ⓕ Ⓖ Ⓗ

Go on

Grade 6/Unit 1 Review Test

11. The plot of the <u>novel</u> was <u>shrewd</u> and <u>abstract</u>.
          A   B   C

11. Ⓐ Ⓑ Ⓒ NONE Ⓓ

12. Don't <u>omit</u> the <u>groove</u> in the road on the <u>peninsula</u>.
      E   F   G

12. Ⓔ Ⓕ Ⓖ NONE Ⓗ

13. I don't <u>denie</u> that my tire, <u>likewise</u>, made a <u>groove</u>.
        A   B   C

13. Ⓐ Ⓑ Ⓒ NONE Ⓓ

14. I am <u>keen</u> on reading a <u>tropical</u> adventure <u>novil</u>.
      E   F   G

14. Ⓔ Ⓕ Ⓖ NONE Ⓗ

15. They did not <u>omit</u> playing the <u>obo</u> at the <u>funeral</u>.
        A   B   C

15. Ⓐ Ⓑ Ⓒ NONE Ⓓ

16. I will <u>devote</u> myself to pouring <u>nectar</u> into the <u>gruve</u>.
     E   F   G

16. Ⓔ Ⓕ Ⓖ NONE Ⓗ

17. The <u>shrewd</u> sailor could <u>casually</u> <u>nafigate</u> at sea.
      A   B   C

17. Ⓐ Ⓑ Ⓒ NONE Ⓓ

18. Before <u>curfew</u> people on the <u>isle</u> <u>bathe</u>.
      E   F G

18. Ⓔ Ⓕ Ⓖ NONE Ⓗ

19. The <u>brilliant</u> boy's <u>scheam</u> was very <u>shrewd.</u>
      A   B   C

19. Ⓐ Ⓑ Ⓒ NONE Ⓓ

20. Don't <u>deny</u> it! A bee cannot <u>omitt</u> taking <u>nectar</u>.
      E   F   G

20. Ⓔ Ⓕ Ⓖ NONE Ⓗ

21. If you <u>bath</u> an <u>oboe</u>, it will get <u>spongy</u> and ruined.
      A   B   C

21. Ⓐ Ⓑ Ⓒ NONE Ⓓ

22. They will <u>navigate</u> around the <u>tropicul</u> <u>lighthouse</u>.
        E   F   G

22. Ⓔ Ⓕ Ⓖ NONE Ⓗ

23. My <u>niece</u> <u>exlaimed</u> that <u>curfew</u> time had past.
     A   B   C

23. Ⓐ Ⓑ Ⓒ NONE Ⓓ

24. He will <u>devote</u> his time to attending a <u>funeral</u> on the <u>isle</u>.
     E   F   G

24. Ⓔ Ⓕ Ⓖ NONE Ⓗ

25. He <u>exclaimed</u> that, <u>likewise</u>, he was <u>kene</u> to depart.
     A   B   C

25. Ⓐ Ⓑ Ⓒ NONE Ⓓ

Syllable Patterns

Pretest Directions

Fold back the paper along the dotted line. Use the blanks to write each word as it is read aloud. When you finish the test, unfold the paper. Use the list at the right to correct any spelling mistakes. Practice the words you missed for the Posttest.

To Parents

Here are the results of your child's weekly spelling Pretest. You can help your child study for the Posttest by following these simple steps for each word on the word list:

1. Read the word to your child.

2. Have your child write the word, saying each letter as it is written.

3. Say each letter of the word as your child checks the spelling.

4. If a mistake has been made, have your child read each letter of the correctly spelled word aloud, and then repeat steps 1–3.

1. _____	1. costume
2. _____	2. pilot
3. _____	3. ragged
4. _____	4. hydrants
5. _____	5. tremble
6. _____	6. profit
7. _____	7. unite
8. _____	8. pirate
9. _____	9. decent
10. _____	10. factor
11. _____	11. panic
12. _____	12. wintry
13. _____	13. vital
14. _____	14. recent
15. _____	15. frustrate
16. _____	16. clutters
17. _____	17. census
18. _____	18. suffix
19. _____	19. pronoun
20. _____	20. minus

Challenge Words

_____ desolate

_____ essay

_____ exaggerated

_____ fidgeted

_____ somberly

Syllable Patterns

Using the Word Study Steps

1. LOOK at the word
2. SAY the word aloud.
3. STUDY the letters in the word.
4. WRITE the word.
5. CHECK the word.

   Did you spell the word right?
   If not, go back to step 1.

Spelling Tip

Look for word chunks that help you remember the spelling of words. Sometimes there may be smaller words in a longer word that will help you to spell it.

cens + **us** = census

hydr + **ants** = hydrants

What's Missing?

Fill in the missing letters to form spelling words.

1. cost ____ m ____
2. pi ____ ____ ____
3. ____ ____ ____ ged
4. hydr ____ ____ ____ s
5. tremb ____ ____
6. pro ____ ____ ____
7. un ____ t ____
8. pi ____ ____ ____ e
9. de ____ ____ ____ ____
10. fact ____ ____

11. ____ ____ ____ ic
12. ____ ____ ____ try
13. vit ____ ____
14. re ____ ____ ____ ____
15. f ____ ____ ____ ____ rate
16. clu ____ ____ ers
17. cens ____ ____
18. suf ____ ____ ____
19. ____ ____ ____ noun
20. min ____ ____

To Parents or Helpers:

Using the Word Study Steps above as your child comes across any new words will help him or her spell words effectively. Review the steps as you both go over this week's spelling words.

Go over the Spelling Tip with your child. Have him or her look for smaller words within the spelling words, such as ragged and profit.

Help your child complete the spelling activity by filling in the missing letters.

Syllable Patterns

costume	tremble	decent	vital	census
pilot	profit	factor	recent	suffix
ragged	unite	panic	frustrate	pronoun
hydrants	pirate	wintry	clutters	minus

Say each word and listen for the vowel sound in the first syllable. Write the words which have the following sounds in the first syllable:

Short vowel sound

1. _____
2. _____
3. _____
4. _____
5. _____
6. _____
7. _____
8. _____
9. _____
10. _____
11. _____

Long vowel sound

12. _____
13. _____
14. _____
15. _____
16. _____
17. _____
18. _____
19. _____
20. _____

Syllable Patterns

costume	tremble	decent	vital	census
pilot	profit	factor	recent	suffix
ragged	unite	panic	frustrate	pronoun
hydrants	pirate	wintry	clutters	minus

Synonym Search

Write the spelling word that is a synonym for each word below.

1. outfit _____

2. tattered _____

3. shake _____

4. gain _____

5. join _____

6. proper _____

7. alarm _____

8. cold _____

9. necessary _____

10. disappoint _____

11. litters _____

12. less _____

Finish the Sentence

Write the spelling word that best completes each sentence.

13. The _____ guided the plane to safety.

14. The fire _____ spilled water into the street.

15. Captain Hook is the _____ captain in *Peter Pan*.

16. An increase in rent was a _____ in our decision to move.

17. A _____ is an official count of the population.

18. Which _____ was added to this word?

19. The teacher asked us to identify which _____ replaced the noun.

20. They told us of the most _____ developments in the project.

36

Challenge Extension: Have students use each Challenge Word in a sentence. Suggest that they use dictionaries to verify meanings.

Grade 6/Unit 2 `20`
Last Summer with Maizon

Syllable Patterns

Proofreading Activity

There are six spelling mistakes in the paragraph below. Circle each misspelled word. Write the words correctly on the lines below.

Margaret and Maizon rode in silence for the last part of the trip. Although autumn had barely begun, the day felt wintrey. As they said goodbye, Margaret saw her friend trembel. It was probably a last-minute pannic about being apart after spending the entire summer together. Maizon felt Margaret tug on her favorite raged sweater as they embraced again. As Margaret watched Maizon walk away, all their rescent times together flashed before her eyes. Later, Margaret wrote a poem about her feelings. At first she only managed to frustate herself. Fortunately, the words soon came easily.

1. _____   3. _____   5. _____

2. _____   4. _____   6. _____

Writing Activity

Write a letter Margaret might write to Maizon. Use at least four spelling words.

_____

_____

_____

_____

Syllable Patterns

Look at the words in each set below. One word in each set is spelled correctly. Use a pencil to fill in the circle next to the correct word. Before you begin, look at the sample sets of words. Sample A has been done for you. Do Sample B by yourself. When you are sure you know what to do, you may go on with the rest of the page.

Sample A:
- (A) climet
- (B) climett
- (C) climate ●
- (D) climat

Sample B:
- (E) ficshion
- (F) ficsion
- (G) fition
- (H) fiction

1. (A) sufix
   (B) sufex
   (C) suffix
   (D) suffex

2. (E) censcus
   (F) census
   (G) censis
   (H) cencis

3. (A) fustrate
   (B) frusrate
   (C) frustate
   (D) frustrate

4. (E) hydrants
   (F) hidrants
   (G) hydrents
   (H) hidrents

5. (A) unnite
   (B) unitte
   (C) unite
   (D) unnit

6. (E) vitel
   (F) vittel
   (G) vital
   (H) vitle

7. (A) pilot
   (B) pillot
   (C) pilat
   (D) pillat

8. (E) raggd
   (F) ragged
   (G) ragid
   (H) raggid

9. (A) trimble
   (B) trembel
   (C) tremble
   (D) trimbel

10. (E) proffet
    (F) profet
    (G) proffit
    (H) profit

11. (A) pronoun
    (B) pronnoun
    (C) pronuon
    (D) pronnuon

12. (E) deccint
    (F) decint
    (G) deccent
    (H) decent

13. (A) pyrate
    (B) pirate
    (C) pirute
    (D) pirrate

14. (E) minis
    (F) minnis
    (G) minus
    (H) minnus

15. (A) wintrey
    (B) wintree
    (C) winty
    (D) wintry

16. (E) panec
    (F) panic
    (G) pannic
    (H) pannec

17. (A) factor
    (B) facter
    (C) factur
    (D) factir

18. (E) cluters
    (F) clutters
    (G) cluttrs
    (H) cluttres

19. (A) rescent
    (B) rescint
    (C) recent
    (D) recint

20. (E) custume
    (F) costume
    (G) costum
    (H) caustume

Words with /f/, /k/, and /s/

Pretest Directions
Fold back the paper along the dotted line. Use the blanks to write each word as it is read aloud. When you finish the test, unfold the paper. Use the list at the right to correct any spelling mistakes. Practice the words you missed for the Posttest.

To Parents
Here are the results of your child's weekly spelling Pretest. You can help your child study for the Posttest by following these simple steps for each word on the word list:

1. Read the word to your child.

2. Have your child write the word, saying each letter as it is written.

3. Say each letter of the word as your child checks the spelling.

4. If a mistake has been made, have your child read each letter of the correctly spelled word aloud, and then repeat steps 1–3.

1. _____ 1. laughed
2. _____ 2. stomach
3. _____ 3. scientist
4. _____ 4. scissors
5. _____ 5. enough
6. _____ 6. character
7. _____ 7. geography
8. _____ 8. muscle
9. _____ 9. symphony
10. _____ 10. chemical
11. _____ 11. scent
12. _____ 12. trough
13. _____ 13. phrase
14. _____ 14. orchestra
15. _____ 15. mechanic
16. _____ 16. scenery
17. _____ 17. chord
18. _____ 18. gopher
19. _____ 19. crescent
20. _____ 20. phase

Challenge Words
_____ encounter
_____ grimaced
_____ ordeals
_____ participate
_____ victorious

Name_____ Date_____

Words with /f/, /k/, and /s/

Using the Word Study Steps

1. LOOK at the word.
2. SAY the word aloud.
3. STUDY the letters in the word.
4. WRITE the word.
5. CHECK the word.

   Did you spell the word right?
   If not, go back to step 1.

Spelling Tip

If you're not sure how to spell a word, give it a try. Write the word different ways to see which one looks correct.

~~stomak~~ ~~stomache~~ stomach

~~mussle~~ ~~mustle~~ muscle

Missing Letters

Fill in the missing letters to form spelling words.

1. lau ____ ____ ed
2. stoma ____ ____
3. enou ____ ____
4. geogra ____ ____ y
5. sym ____ ____ ony
6. trou ____ ____
7. or ____ ____ estra
8. me ____ ____ anic
9. go ____ ____ er
10. ____ ____ ientist

11. ____ ____ issors
12. ____ ____ aracter
13. mu ____ ____ le
14. ____ ____ emical
15. ____ ____ ent
16. ____ ____ rase
17. ____ ____ enery
18. ____ ____ ord
19. cre____ ____ ent
20. ____ ____ ase

To Parents or Helpers:

Using the Word Study Steps above as your child comes across any new words will help him or her spell words effectively. Review the steps as you both go over this week's spelling words.

Go over the Spelling Tip with your child. Help your child try to spell out some of the spelling words.

Help your child complete the spelling activity by filling in the missing letters.

Words with /f/, /k/, and /s/

laughed	enough	symphony	phrase	chord
stomach	character	chemical	orchestra	gopher
scientist	geography	scent	mechanic	crescent
scissors	muscle	trough	scenery	phase

Sort each spelling word according to the sound and spelling pattern to which it belongs. Write words with the following spelling patterns:

/f/ spelled

ph

1. _____
2. _____
3. _____
4. _____
5. _____

/f/ spelled

gh

6. _____
7. _____
8. _____

/k/ spelled

ch

9. _____
10. _____
11. _____
12. _____
13. _____
14. _____

/s/ spelled

sc

15. _____
16. _____
17. _____
18. _____
19. _____
20. _____

Words with /f/, /k/, and /s/

laughed	enough	symphony	phrase	chord
stomach	character	chemical	orchestra	gopher
scientist	geography	scent	mechanic	crescent
scissors	muscle	trough	scenery	phase

Meaning Match-Up
Write the spelling word that best matches each definition below.

1. cutting tool _____

2. plenty _____

3. individual nature _____

4. musical composition _____

5. distinctive smell _____

6. long bin _____

7. group of words _____

8. background _____

9. musical tones _____

10. stage _____

Analogies
Write the spelling word which completes each analogy.

11. Giggled is to _____ as **chatted** is to **talked**.

12. Air is to **lungs** as **food** is to _____.

13. Math is to **mathematician** as **science** is to _____.

14. Brain is to **intellect** as _____ is to **strength**.

15. Dentist is to **teeth** as _____ is to **car**.

Completions
Use a spelling word to complete the following sentences.

16. The study of Earth's surface is _____.

17. In our science class, we learned about _____ reactions.

18. A _____ is an animal known for digging tunnels.

19. The conductor directed the _____ as they played.

20. The moon is sometimes shaped like a _____.

Challenge Extension: Have students scramble each Challenge
Word and then have a partner try to unscramble the words.

Name_____ Date_____ **Spelling** 43

Words with /f/, /k/, and /s/

Proofreading Activity

There are six spelling mistakes in the paragraph below. Circle each misspelled word. Write the words correctly on the lines below.

Mary didn't understand why going through the endurance ritual of Ta-Na-E-Ka was important. Perhaps observing the natural world would interest a girl who wanted to be a sientist. But would Ta-Na-E-Ka help a girl become a meckanic and fix trucks? Could it help a boy learn to play a symfony with an orcestra? Besides, how would she find enouph to eat? Would she keep her stumach full by finding a dead deer like Grandfather did? Mary was worried about the whole thing.

1. _____   3. _____   5. _____

2. _____   4. _____   6. _____

Writing Activity

Write a dialogue between Mary and Grandfather about why she should or should not need to participate in Ta-Na-E-Ka. Use at least four spelling words.

_____

_____

_____

_____

Words with /f/, /k/, and /s/

Look at the words in each set below. One word in each set is spelled correctly. Use a pencil to fill in the circle next to the correct word. Before you begin, look at the sample sets of words. Sample A has been done for you. Do Sample B by yourself. When you are sure you know what to do, you may go on with the rest of the page.

Sample A:
- (A) coff
- (B) couf
- (C) cogh
- (D) cough ●

Sample B:
- (E) teknical
- (F) tecknical
- (G) technical
- (H) tecnical

1. (A) gogher
   (B) gohfer
   (C) gopher
   (D) goffer

2. (E) stomich
   (F) stomach
   (G) stumack
   (H) stumick

3. (A) orquestra
   (B) orcestra
   (C) orkestra
   (D) orchestra

4. (E) scientist
   (F) sientist
   (G) sceintist
   (H) seintist

5. (A) laufed
   (B) laffed
   (C) laughed
   (D) lauphed

6. (E) caracter
   (F) carachter
   (G) character
   (H) charicter

7. (A) scissors
   (B) scizzors
   (C) sissors
   (D) sizzors

8. (E) cresent
   (F) crescent
   (G) crescant
   (H) crecent

9. (A) gegraphy
   (B) geograghy
   (C) geography
   (D) geograffy

10. (E) simphony
    (F) symphany
    (G) symghany
    (H) symphony

11. (A) phrase
    (B) phrais
    (C) frase
    (D) fraise

12. (E) trouff
    (F) trogh
    (G) troff
    (H) trough

13. (A) cemical
    (B) chemical
    (C) chemicle
    (D) cemicel

14. (E) mussle
    (F) muscel
    (G) muscle
    (H) mussal

15. (A) kord
    (B) chorde
    (C) coard
    (D) chord

16. (E) meckanic
    (F) mechanic
    (G) mecanic
    (H) machanic

17. (A) scent
    (B) csent
    (C) sint
    (D) cint

18. (E) enouph
    (F) enough
    (G) enouff
    (H) enugh

19. (A) phaze
    (B) fase
    (C) phase
    (D) phaiz

20. (E) seenery
    (F) scenery
    (G) seanery
    (H) scenry

Words with /ou/ and /oi/

Pretest Directions
Fold back the paper along the dotted line. Use the blanks to write each word as it is read aloud. When you finish the test, unfold the paper. Use the list at the right to correct any spelling mistakes. Practice the words you missed for the Posttest.

To Parents
Here are the results of your child's weekly spelling Pretest. You can help your child study for the Posttest by following these simple steps for each word on the word list:

1. Read the word to your child.

2. Have your child write the word, saying each letter as it is written.

3. Say each letter of the word as your child checks the spelling.

4. If a mistake has been made, have your child read each letter of the correctly spelled word aloud, and then repeat steps 1–3.

1. _____	1. coward
2. _____	2. counter
3. _____	3. oyster
4. _____	4. embroidered
5. _____	5. crouch
6. _____	6. employer
7. _____	7. browse
8. _____	8. moisture
9. _____	9. trout
10. _____	10. vowel
11. _____	11. alloy
12. _____	12. poise
13. _____	13. flounder
14. _____	14. nightgowns
15. _____	15. corduroy
16. _____	16. loiter
17. _____	17. blouse
18. _____	18. glowering
19. _____	19. outgrown
20. _____	20. boycott

Challenge Words

_____	exasperated
_____	improvement
_____	pouted
_____	rationed
_____	sophisticated

Words with /ou/ and /oi/

Using the Word Study Steps

1. LOOK at the word.
2. SAY the word aloud.
3. STUDY the letters in the word.
4. WRITE the word.
5. CHECK the word.

   Did you spell the word right?
   If not, go back to step 1.

Spelling Tip

Look for word chunks or smaller words that help you remember the spelling of longer words.

glow   e   ring

Word Scramble

Unscramble the sets of letters below to form spelling words.

1. drawco _____
2. tenrouc _____
3. stoyre _____
4. bremdioreed _____
5. ocruch _____
6. remlyope _____
7. swober _____
8. stoumire _____
9. ottru _____
10. woelv _____

11. loayl _____
12. sipoe _____
13. frednulo _____
14. towngigshn _____
15. drouorcy _____
16. troile _____
17. slobue _____
18. growlenig _____
19. groutnow _____
20. tycoobt _____

To Parents or Helpers:
   Using the Word Study Steps above as your child comes across any new words will help him or her spell words effectively. Review the steps as you both go over this week's spelling words.

   Go over the Spelling Tip with your child. Help your child find smaller words or word chunks in some of the longer spelling words.

   Help your child complete the Spelling Activity by unscrambling each set of letters to form a spelling word.

Words with /ou/ and /oi/

coward	crouch	trout	flounder	blouse
counter	employer	vowel	nightgowns	glowering
oyster	browse	alloy	corduroy	outgrown
embroidered	moisture	poise	loiter	boycott

Sort each spelling word according to the sound and spelling pattern it contains.
Write the words with /ou/ spelled as follows:

ou

1. _____
2. _____
3. _____
4. _____
5. _____
6. _____

ow

7. _____
8. _____
9. _____
10. _____
11. _____

Write the words with /oi/ spelled as follows:

oy

12. _____
13. _____
14. _____
15. _____
16. _____

oi

17. _____
18. _____
19. _____
20. _____

Words with /ou/ and /oi/

coward	crouch	trout	flounder	blouse
counter	employer	vowel	nightgowns	glowering
oyster	browse	alloy	corduroy	outgrown
embroidered	moisture	poise	loiter	boycott

Synonym Search

Write the spelling word that is a synonym for each word below.

1. tabletop _____

2. decorated _____

3. stoop _____

4. glance _____

5. dampness _____

6. composure _____

7. struggle _____

8. linger _____

9. shirt _____

10. scowling _____

Antonyms

Write the spelling word that is the opposite of each word below.

11. consonant _____

12. employee _____

Definitions

Write the spelling word that best matches each definition below.

13. a person who lacks courage _____

14. a member of the mollusk family _____

15. a type of fish related to salmon _____

16. a combination of metals _____

17. loose garments worn to bed _____

18. fabric with a velvety, ribbed surface _____

19. grown too large for _____

20. to refuse to have dealings with _____

Challenge Extension: Have students write a
paragraph using the Challenge Words.

Grade 6/Unit 2
Number the Stars 20

Name_____ Date_____ **Spelling**

Words with /ou/ and /oi/

Proofreading Activity

There are six spelling mistakes in the paragraph below. Circle each misspelled word. Write the words correctly on the lines below.

The girls were in their nightgouns when they heard the heavy knock. Mamma was drying the dishes, with an embroydered towel. Laying it down on the cownter she answered the door. A glouering soldier asked where the Rosens were. Annemarie was not a couard but she was frightened. Ellen was frightened, too, but she managed to keep her poyse and answer the soldier's questions.

1. _____   3. _____   5. _____

2. _____   4. _____   6. _____

Writing Activity

Write a paragraph about a situation where you were frightened but had to maintain your composure. Use four spelling words.

_____

_____

_____

_____

Words with /ou/ and /oi/

Look at the words in each set below. One word in each set is spelled correctly. Use a pencil to fill in the circle next to the correct word. Before you begin, look at the sample sets of words. Sample A has been done for you. Do Sample B by yourself. When you are sure you know what to do, you may go on with the rest of the page.

Sample A:
- Ⓐ grownd
- Ⓑ grounnd
- ● ground
- Ⓓ grownde

Sample B:
- Ⓔ joifull
- Ⓕ joyfull
- Ⓖ joiful
- Ⓗ joyful

1. Ⓐ emploier
Ⓑ employer
Ⓒ employr
Ⓓ emploir

2. Ⓔ crowch
Ⓕ crowtch
Ⓖ crouch
Ⓗ croutch

3. Ⓐ brouse
Ⓑ brous
Ⓒ browze
Ⓓ browse

4. Ⓔ embroidered
Ⓕ embroydered
Ⓖ imbroidered
Ⓗ imbroydered

5. Ⓐ oister
Ⓑ oiscter
Ⓒ oyster
Ⓓ oyscter

6. Ⓔ cownter
Ⓕ cowntr
Ⓖ counter
Ⓗ countr

7. Ⓐ moisture
Ⓑ moysture
Ⓒ moistere
Ⓓ moystere

8. Ⓔ flownder
Ⓕ flounder
Ⓖ flouder
Ⓗ flowder

9. Ⓐ poize
Ⓑ poyze
Ⓒ poise
Ⓓ poyse

10. Ⓔ nightgouns
Ⓕ nitegouns
Ⓖ nightgowns
Ⓗ nitegowns

11. Ⓐ alloy
Ⓑ alloi
Ⓒ aloy
Ⓓ aloi

12. Ⓔ corduroi
Ⓕ corduroy
Ⓖ corderoy
Ⓗ corduroi

13. Ⓐ vouel
Ⓑ vowel
Ⓒ vowl
Ⓓ voul

14. Ⓔ troot
Ⓕ truot
Ⓖ trout
Ⓗ trowt

15. Ⓐ loyter
Ⓑ loytur
Ⓒ loitur
Ⓓ loiter

16. Ⓔ outgroun
Ⓕ outgrown
Ⓖ owtgrown
Ⓗ owtgroun

17. Ⓐ glowering
Ⓑ glowerring
Ⓒ glouering
Ⓓ glouerring

18. Ⓔ boycot
Ⓕ boycott
Ⓖ boicot
Ⓗ boicott

19. Ⓐ couard
Ⓑ courd
Ⓒ coward
Ⓓ cowerd

20. Ⓔ blowes
Ⓕ blous
Ⓖ blowse
Ⓗ blouse

Plurals

Pretest Directions
Fold back the paper along the dotted line. Use the blanks to write each word as it is read aloud. When you finish the test, unfold the paper. Use the list at the right to correct any spelling mistakes. Practice the words you missed for the Posttest.

To Parents
Here are the results of your child's weekly spelling Pretest. You can help your child study for the Posttest by following these simple steps for each word on the word list:

1. Read the word to your child.

2. Have your child write the word, saying each letter as it is written.

3. Say each letter of the word as your child checks the spelling.

4. If a mistake has been made, have your child read each letter of the correctly spelled word aloud, and then repeat steps 1–3.

1. _____	1. memories
2. _____	2. ashes
3. _____	3. mysteries
4. _____	4. volcanoes
5. _____	5. notches
6. _____	6. solos
7. _____	7. cuffs
8. _____	8. buffaloes
9. _____	9. earmuffs
10. _____	10. abilities
11. _____	11. scarves
12. _____	12. concertos
13. _____	13. industries
14. _____	14. dominoes
15. _____	15. flamingos
16. _____	16. halves
17. _____	17. sheriffs
18. _____	18. stereos
19. _____	19. patios
20. _____	20. wharves

Challenge Words

_____	cultivate
_____	diminished
_____	devised
_____	edible
_____	retrieved

Name_____ Date_____

Plurals

Using the Word Study Steps

1. LOOK at the word.
2. SAY the word aloud.
3. STUDY the letters in the word.
4. WRITE the word.
5. CHECK the word.

   Did you spell the word right?
   If not, go back to step 1.

Spelling Tip

To change plural words ending in -*ves* back to singular, you need to delete -*es* and change the *v* to *f* or *fe*.

wharves = wharf
lives = life

Word Scramble

Unscramble each set of letters to make a spelling word.

1. covonlase _____
2. farefums _____
3. chenots _____
4. estymseri _____
5. semorime _____
6. sesha _____
7. fcsuf _____
8. estrinisud _____
9. glinafsmo _____
10. taiblisie _____

11. flofabues _____
12. torscenco _____
13. rascevs _____
14. vawhers _____
15. losso _____
16. satipo _____
17. fershifs _____
18. nodosmie _____
19. veshal _____
20. osterse _____

To Parents or Helpers:

Using the Word Study Steps above as your child comes across any new words will help him or her spell words effectively. Review the steps as you both go over this week's spelling words.

Go over the Spelling Tip with your child. Try to help your student recognize other patterns when forming plurals.

Help your child unscramble the spelling words.

Plurals

memories	notches	earmuffs	industries	sheriffs
ashes	solos	abilities	dominoes	stereos
mysteries	cuffs	scarves	flamingos	patios
volcanoes	buffaloes	concertos	halves	wharves

Sort each spelling word according to the spelling pattern to which it belongs. Write the words with the following endings:

-es

1. _____

2. _____

-ies

3. _____

4. _____

5. _____

6. _____

-os

7. _____

8. _____

9. _____

10. _____

11. _____

-oes

12. _____

13. _____

14. _____

-fs

15. _____

16. _____

17. _____

-ves

18. _____

19. _____

20. _____

Plurals

memories	notches	earmuffs	industries	sheriffs
ashes	solos	abilities	dominoes	stereos
mysteries	cuffs	scarves	flamingos	patios
volcanoes	buffaloes	concertos	halves	wharves

Categories
Write a spelling word to complete each of these word groups.

1. comedies   dramas _____

2. earthquakes   avalanches _____

3. nicks   cuts _____

4. collars   sleeves _____

5. radios   televisions _____

Definitions
Write the spelling word which matches each definition below.

6. remembered things _____   **11.** capacities _____

7. burned remnants _____   **12.** manufacturers _____

8. done alone _____   **13.** law officers _____

9. bison _____   **14.** terraces _____

10. ear coverings _____   **15.** docks _____

Sentence Completions
Write the spelling word which best completes each sentence.

16. When it turned cold, we put _____ around our necks.

17. We listened to the _____ performed by the orchestra.

18. The old men played _____ in the park.

19. All the cakes were divided into _____.

20. In Florida, she saw several pink _____.

Challenge Extension: Have students work with a
partner to create a dictionary page with entries for the
Challenge Words.

54

Grade 6/Unit 2
Opera, Karate, and Bandits

20

Plurals

Proofreading Activity

There are six spelling mistakes in the paragraph below. Circle each misspelled word. Write the words correctly on the lines below.

The narrator shares his childhood memorys of Vietnam. There were many wild animals, such as crocodiles and water buffeloes. They had no modern conveniences like radios or stereoes, and no major industrys. When the war reduced many hamlets to ashs, the narrator left Vietnam. Fortunately, his creative abilityes brought him success in the United States.

1. _____   3. _____   5. _____

2. _____   4. _____   6. _____

Writing Activity

Suppose someone wrote about childhood memories of your town or neighborhood. Write some details that might be included. Use at least four spelling words.

_____

_____

_____

_____

Plurals

Look at the words in each set below. One word in each set is spelled correctly. Use a pencil to fill in the circle next to the correct word. Before you begin, look at the sample sets of words. Sample A has been done for you. Do Sample B by yourself. When you are sure you know what to do, you may go on with the rest of the page.

Sample A:
- (A) maches
- (B) matchs
- (C) matshes
- (D) matches ●

Sample B:
- (E) candeys
- (F) candys
- (G) candies
- (H) candyies

1.
- (A) flumingos
- (B) flumingoes
- (C) flamingos
- (D) flammingos

2.
- (E) patioes
- (F) patios
- (G) pateos
- (H) patteos

3.
- (A) earmuves
- (B) earmufves
- (C) earmufs
- (D) earmuffs

4.
- (E) volcanoes
- (F) vulcanoes
- (G) volcannoes
- (H) voulcanoes

5.
- (A) noches
- (B) nochs
- (C) notches
- (D) notchs

6.
- (E) mystries
- (F) mystryes
- (G) mysteries
- (H) mysteryes

7.
- (A) solos
- (B) soloes
- (C) sollos
- (D) solloes

8.
- (E) ashs
- (F) ashes
- (G) asches
- (H) aschs

9.
- (A) cufves
- (B) cuves
- (C) cuffs
- (D) cufs

10.
- (E) memorys
- (F) memoreys
- (G) memoryes
- (H) memories

11.
- (A) buffaloes
- (B) buffiloes
- (C) bufaloes
- (D) bufiloes

12.
- (E) halfes
- (F) halfs
- (G) halvs
- (H) halves

13.
- (A) domenoes
- (B) dominoes
- (C) domminoes
- (D) dominnoes

14.
- (E) sherifves
- (F) sherives
- (G) sheriffs
- (H) sherifs

15.
- (A) industrys
- (B) industryes
- (C) industreys
- (D) industries

16.
- (E) stereoes
- (F) stereos
- (G) steroes
- (H) sterios

17.
- (A) concertos
- (B) concertoes
- (C) conchertos
- (D) conciertos

18.
- (E) scarfes
- (F) scarves
- (G) scarffs
- (H) scarvs

19.
- (A) abiliteys
- (B) abilitys
- (C) abilities
- (D) abilitis

20.
- (E) wharvs
- (F) wharves
- (G) wharfes
- (H) wharffs

Words from the Arts

Pretest Directions

Fold back the paper along the dotted line. Use the blanks to write each word as it is read aloud. When you finish the test, unfold the paper. Use the list at the right to correct any spelling mistakes. Practice the words you missed for the Posttest.

To Parents

Here are the results of your child's weekly spelling Pretest. You can help your child study for the Posttest by following these simple steps for each word on the word list:

1. Read the word to your child.

2. Have your child write the word, saying each letter as it is written.

3. Say each letter of the word as your child checks the spelling.

4. If a mistake has been made, have your child read each letter of the correctly spelled word aloud, and then repeat steps 1–3.

#		Word
1.	_____	1. terrace
2.	_____	2. palace
3.	_____	3. classical
4.	_____	4. landscape
5.	_____	5. fountains
6.	_____	6. temples
7.	_____	7. pavements
8.	_____	8. structure
9.	_____	9. traditional
10.	_____	10. exotic
11.	_____	11. mosaic
12.	_____	12. artifact
13.	_____	13. pyramid
14.	_____	14. estate
15.	_____	15. primary
16.	_____	16. dimension
17.	_____	17. representation
18.	_____	18. pillars
19.	_____	19. extension
20.	_____	20. architecture

Challenge Words

_____ cobblestone

_____ romance

_____ splendors

_____ surprisingly

_____ undersea

Name_____ Date_____ **Spelling**

Words from the Arts

Using the Word Study Steps

1. LOOK at the word
2. SAY the word aloud.
3. STUDY the letters in the word.
4. WRITE the word.
5. CHECK the word.

   Did you spell the word right?
   If not, go back to step 1.

Spelling Tip

Look for word chunks or smaller words that help you remember the spelling of longer words.

class i cal
ar ti **fact**
re **present** a tion

Find and Circle

Find and circle the spelling words in this puzzle.

```
b e u k t e r r a c e a n p a l a c e n u m e t i r x
c l a s s i c a l h a r l a n d s c a p e a n p r e i b
f a u f o u n t a i n s t e r m t e m p l e s e r n b i
t e m p e l s p a v e m e n t s s t r u c t u r e d n
t r a g k h i o n e l e x o t i c a n i m o s a i c a r i t
a r t i f i c a r t i f a c t h w p y r a m i d e s t a y n
e s t a t e c h i b h u r k n l e u t r a d i t i o n a l
n e u f a n l i r n o p e r a n u j i k m p r i m a r y
```

To Parents or Helpers:
   Using the Word Study Steps above as your child comes across any new words will help him or her spell well. Review the steps as you both go over this week's spelling words.
   Go over the Spelling Tip with your child. Help your child divide other spelling words into word chunks.
   Help your child complete the Spelling Activity by finding and circling the spelling words in the puzzle.

Words from the Arts

terrace	fountains	traditional	pyramid	representation
palace	temples	exotic	estate	pillars
classical	pavements	mosaic	primary	extension
landscape	structure	artifact	dimension	architecture

Alphabetical Order

Write the spelling words in alphabetical order.

1. _____

2. _____

3. _____

4. _____

5. _____

6. _____

7. _____

8. _____

9. _____

10. _____

11. _____

12. _____

13. _____

14. _____

15. _____

16. _____

17. _____

18. _____

19. _____

20. _____

Words from the Arts

terrace	fountains	traditional	pyramid	representation
palace	temples	exotic	estate	pillars
classical	pavements	mosaic	primary	extension
landscape	structure	artifact	dimension	architecture

Definitions

Write the spelling word which best matches each definition below.

1. official residence of royalty _____

2. buildings dedicated to worship _____

3. road or sidewalk coverings _____

4. decoration made of inlaid stones or glass _____

5. a building with a square base and four triangular sides _____

6. a measurable extent _____

7. a picture or likeness that symbolizes something _____

8. the science or art of the construction of buildings _____

Sentence Completions

Use a spelling word to complete each sentence.

9. The water squirted from the _____ in the town square.

10. An _____ may be a tool from an ancient civilization.

11. That building has lovely _____ which help support it.

12. We added a two-room _____ to our house.

Challenge Extension: Have students write a completion
sentence for each Challenge Word. Then have students
exchange papers and complete the sentences.

Grade 6/Unit 2
Cleopatra's Lost Palace 12

Words from the Arts

Proofreading Activity

There are six spelling mistakes in the paragraph below. Circle each misspelled word. Write the words correctly on the lines below.

Alexander the Great built Alexandria after seeing the beautiful landskape of the harbor. The city was decorated with many tempels, gardens, and fountins. Cleopatra's grand palase stood on Antirhodos, near Alexandria. Antirhodos is now buried underwater due to floods and earthquakes. Explorers have recently uncovered statues, pillers, and other artifactes that may have been part of Cleopatra's world.

1. _____ 3. _____ 5. _____

2. _____ 4. _____ 6. _____

Writing Activity

Write a possible description of Alexandria. Use at least four spelling words.

_____

_____

_____

_____

Words from the Arts

Look at the words in each set below. One word in each set is spelled correctly. Use a pencil to fill in the circle next to the correct word. Before you begin, look at the sample sets of words. Sample A has been done for you. Do Sample B by yourself. When you are sure you know what to do, you may go on with the rest of the page.

Sample A:
- (A) museim
- (B) muzeum
- (C) musiem
- (D) museum ●

Sample B:
- (E) rooins
- (F) ruens
- (G) ruins
- (H) ryuins

1.
(A) terace
(B) terrace
(C) terrase
(D) terase

2.
(E) pallace
(F) palase
(G) palace
(H) palice

3.
(A) clasical
(B) classicel
(C) classicle
(D) classical

4.
(E) landskape
(F) landscape
(G) landsceape
(H) landsceap

5.
(A) fountains
(B) fountins
(C) fowntains
(D) fountens

6.
(E) temples
(F) tempels
(G) tempils
(H) tempeles

7.
(A) payvements
(B) pavemints
(C) pavements
(D) pavemants

8.
(E) struckture
(F) structir
(G) structure
(H) structcher

9.
(A) tradisional
(B) traditional
(C) tradishional
(D) traditionel

10.
(E) exatic
(F) exotic
(G) ecsotic
(H) exsotic

11.
(A) mozaic
(B) mosaic
(C) mosiac
(D) mosaik

12.
(E) artifact
(F) artefact
(G) artifakt
(H) artufact

13.
(A) piramid
(B) pryamidl
(C) pyrimad
(D) pyramid

14.
(E) astate
(F) estait
(G) ehstate
(H) estate

15.
(A) primary
(B) prymary
(C) primerry
(D) primery

16.
(E) dimention
(F) damension
(G) dimension
(H) dimmension

17.
(A) representaytion
(B) reprisentation
(C) representasion
(D) representation

18.
(E) pillers
(F) pillars
(G) pilars
(H) pellars

19.
(A) extension
(B) extention
(C) extendsion
(D) extinsion

20.
(E) arcitecture
(F) arkitecture
(G) architecture
(H) arkhitecture

Grade 6/Unit 2 Review Test

Read each sentence. If an underlined word is spelled wrong, fill in the circle that goes with that word. If no word is spelled wrong, fill in the circle below NONE.

Read Sample A and do Sample B.

A. Rosa and her mother have <u>different</u> <u>tastes</u> in <u>cloze</u>.
                             A   **B**   **C**

                NONE
A. Ⓐ Ⓑ ● Ⓓ

B. He had <u>memmories</u> of the water <u>buffaloes</u> in the <u>hamlet</u>.
               E   **F**   **G**

                NONE
B. Ⓔ Ⓕ Ⓖ Ⓗ

1. The <u>decent</u> man took a <u>census</u> on the <u>terrace</u>.
       A   **B**   **C**

                NONE
1. Ⓐ Ⓑ Ⓒ Ⓓ

2. The <u>wintery</u> weather impedes the <u>abilities</u> of the <u>flamingos</u>.
          E   **F**   **G**

                NONE
2. Ⓔ Ⓕ Ⓖ Ⓗ

3. The fire <u>hidrants</u> near the <u>wharves</u> have <u>notches</u>.
            A   **B**   **C**

                NONE
3. Ⓐ Ⓑ Ⓒ Ⓓ

4. The <u>orkestra</u> playing the <u>symphony</u> had great <u>poise</u>.
         E   **F**   **G**

                NONE
4. Ⓔ Ⓕ Ⓖ Ⓗ

5. I found an <u>exotic</u> <u>oister</u> in the <u>trough</u>.
                A   **B**   **C**

                NONE
5. Ⓐ Ⓑ Ⓒ Ⓓ

6. The <u>artifact</u> in the <u>pyramid</u> was shaped like a <u>cressent</u>.
        E   **F**   **G**

                NONE
6. Ⓔ Ⓕ Ⓖ Ⓗ

7. The <u>glowering</u> man made me <u>crouch</u> down on the <u>terrace</u>.
          A   **B**   **C**

                NONE
7. Ⓐ Ⓑ Ⓒ Ⓓ

8. Whoever <u>embroidered</u> this <u>exotik</u> purse has great <u>abilities</u>.
               E   **F**   **G**

                NONE
8. Ⓔ Ⓕ Ⓖ Ⓗ

9. The <u>volcanos</u> destroyed the <u>wharves</u> and the fire <u>hydrants</u>.
          A   **B**   **C**

                NONE
9. Ⓐ Ⓑ Ⓒ Ⓓ

10. That <u>mosaic</u> on the <u>terrace</u> is an ancient <u>artifact</u>.
          E   **F**   **G**

                NONE
10. Ⓔ Ⓕ Ⓖ Ⓗ

Go on →

Grade 6/Unit 2 Review Test

11. The <u>orchestra</u> made a <u>desent</u> <u>profit</u>.
    A   B   C
11. Ⓐ   Ⓑ   Ⓒ   NONE Ⓓ

12. The <u>wintry</u> mist covered the <u>wharfs</u> and <u>terrace</u>.
    E   F   G
12. Ⓔ   Ⓕ   Ⓖ   NONE Ⓗ

13. The <u>exotic</u> <u>flamingos</u> had <u>poise</u>.
    A   B   C
13. Ⓐ   Ⓑ   Ⓒ   NONE Ⓓ

14. The <u>kord</u> in that <u>symphony</u> sounds <u>decent</u>.
    E   F   G
14. Ⓔ   Ⓕ   Ⓖ   NONE Ⓗ

15. She left her <u>embroidered</u> purse in the <u>troff</u> near the <u>hydrants</u>.
             A   B   C
15. Ⓐ   Ⓑ   Ⓒ   NONE Ⓓ

16. The members of the <u>orchestra</u> have <u>decent</u> <u>abilites</u>.
               E   F   G
16. Ⓔ   Ⓕ   Ⓖ   NONE Ⓗ

17. The <u>crescent</u> <u>mosaic</u> is on the <u>terrase</u>.
    A   B   C
17. Ⓐ   Ⓑ   Ⓒ   NONE Ⓓ

18. <u>Crowch</u> behind the <u>pyramid</u> to see the <u>volcanoes</u>.
    E   F   G
18. Ⓔ   Ⓕ   Ⓖ   NONE Ⓗ

19. A <u>glowering</u> cat is on the <u>embroydered</u> <u>artifact</u>.
     A   B   C
19. Ⓐ   Ⓑ   Ⓒ   NONE Ⓓ

20. The <u>sensus</u> says <u>volcanoes</u> won't occur in <u>wintry</u> weather.
    E   F   G
20. Ⓔ   Ⓕ   Ⓖ   NONE Ⓗ

21. The <u>oyster</u> will bring less <u>profit</u> than the <u>flamingos</u>.
     A   B   C
21. Ⓐ   Ⓑ   Ⓒ   NONE Ⓓ

22. A <u>decent</u> artist carved <u>noches</u> on the <u>wharves</u>.
    E   F   G
22. Ⓔ   Ⓕ   Ⓖ   NONE Ⓗ

23. The <u>orchestra</u> played the wrong <u>chord</u> during the <u>symphony</u>.
     A   B   C
23. Ⓐ   Ⓑ   Ⓒ   NONE Ⓓ

24. There is an <u>exotic</u> <u>mozaic</u> in the <u>pyramid</u>.
        E   F   G
24. Ⓔ   Ⓕ   Ⓖ   NONE Ⓗ

25. The <u>oyster</u> in the <u>trough</u> had <u>notches</u> on it.
    A   B   C
25. Ⓐ   Ⓑ   Ⓒ   NONE Ⓓ

Words with /ô/ and /ôr/

Pretest Directions

Fold back the paper along the dotted line. Use the blanks to write each word as it is read aloud. When you finish the test, unfold the paper. Use the list at the right to correct any spelling mistakes. Practice the words you missed for the Posttest.

To Parents

Here are the results of your child's weekly spelling Pretest. You can help your child study for the Posttest by following these simple steps for each word on the word list:

1. Read the word to your child.

2. Have your child write the word, saying each letter as it is written.

3. Say each letter of the word as your child checks the spelling.

4. If a mistake has been made, have your child read each letter of the correctly spelled word aloud, and then repeat steps 1–3.

#		Word
1.	_____	1. pause
2.	_____	2. sword
3.	_____	3. walrus
4.	_____	4. warp
5.	_____	5. mourn
6.	_____	6. ignore
7.	_____	7. ought
8.	_____	8. fork
9.	_____	9. laundry
10.	_____	10. lawyer
11.	_____	11. sort
12.	_____	12. faucet
13.	_____	13. foresee
14.	_____	14. wardrobe
15.	_____	15. core
16.	_____	16. wharf
17.	_____	17. almanac
18.	_____	18. resource
19.	_____	19. thoughtless
20.	_____	20. flaw

Challenge Words

_____ diagonal

_____ inquisitive

_____ painstakingly

_____ unconsciously

_____ visual

Words with /ô/ and /ôr/

Using the Word Study Steps

1. LOOK at the word.
2. SAY the word aloud.
3. STUDY the letters in the word.
4. WRITE the word.
5. CHECK the word.

   Did you spell the word right?
   If not, go back to step 1.

Spelling Tip

Look for word chunks or smaller words that help you remember the spelling of the word.

thought + less = thoughtless

law + yer = lawyer

Find Rhyming Words

Circle the word in each row that rhymes with the spelling word on the left.

1.	**pause**	jaws	please	praise
2.	**mourn**	mean	mow	torn
3.	**fork**	stork	freak	flick
4.	**ignore**	ignite	restore	glory
5.	**flaw**	flight	flew	raw
6.	**ought**	thought	enough	bright
7.	**sword**	cord	card	swore
8.	**resource**	result	enforce	recent
9.	**sort**	fort	source	sorry
10.	**core**	care	floor	crow

To Parents or Helpers:

   Using the Word Study Steps above as your child comes across any new words will help him or her spell words effectively. Review the steps as you both go over this week's spelling words.

   Go over the Spelling Tip with your child. Have him or her find words that contain small words or word chunks. Help your child complete the spelling activity.

Name_____ Date_____

Words with /ô/ and /ôr/

pause	mourn	laundry	foresee	almanac
sword	ignore	lawyer	wardrobe	resource
walrus	ought	sort	core	thoughtless
warp	fork	faucet	wharf	flaw

Sort each spelling word according to the sound and spelling pattern to which it belongs.
Write the words with /ô/ spelled as follows:

au

1. _____

2. _____

3. _____

aw

4. _____

5. _____

a

6. _____

7. _____

ough

8. _____

9. _____

Write the words with /ôr/ spelled as follows:

or

10. _____

11. _____

12. _____

ar

13. _____

14. _____

15. _____

ore

16. _____

17. _____

18. _____

our

19. _____

20. _____

Words with /ô/ and /ôr/

pause	mourn	laundry	foresee	almanac
sword	ignore	lawyer	wardrobe	resource
walrus	ought	sort	core	thoughtless
warp	fork	faucet	wharf	flaw

Word Meaning: Analogies

Fill in the spelling word that fits the meaning of the analogy.

1. *fern* is to *plant* as _____ is to *animal*

2. *pit* is to *peach* as _____ is to *apple*

3. *books* are to *library* as *clothes* are to _____

4. *metal* is to *rust* as *wood* is to _____

5. *classroom* is to *teacher* as *courtroom* is to _____

6. *pen* is to *pencil* as *spoon* is to _____

7. *wedding* is to *rejoice* as *funeral* is to _____

8. *boat* is to *ship* as *dock* is to _____

Synonyms and Antonyms

Write a spelling word that is a synonym (S) or antonym (A) for each word below.

9. thoughtful (A) _____

10. delay (S) _____

11. weapon (S) _____

12. regard (A) _____

13. wash (S) _____

14. kind (S) _____

15. valve (S) _____

16. predict (S) _____

17. waste (A) _____

18. blemish (S) _____

19. calendar (S) _____

20. should (S) _____

Challenge Extension: Write one fill-in sentence for each Challenge Word. Exchange papers with a partner and complete the sentences.

Grade 6/Unit 3
Boy of Unusual Vision

20

Words with /ô/ and /ôr/

Proofreading Activity

There are six spelling mistakes in the paragraph below. Circle the misspelled words. Write the words correctly on the lines below.

Even though he is blind, Calvin helps his mother take care of the house. After dinner, he washes his own dishes. He holds them under the foucet and scrubs them with a brush. After drying them, he helps soart and put away his plate, spoon, knife, and forke. Calvin also helps do the lawndry. He is such a good helper, his mother never has to tell him what he aught to do. She can't forsee a day when he won't be glad to help out.

1. _____   3. _____   5. _____

2. _____   4. _____   6. _____

Writing Activity

Do you help to take care of your house or your room? Write about how you help out at home. Use four spelling words in your writing.

_____

_____

_____

_____

Words with /ô/ and /ôr/

Look at the words in each set below. One word in each set is spelled correctly. Use a pencil to fill in the circle next to the correct word. Before you begin, look at the sample sets of words. Sample A has been done for you. Do Sample B by yourself. When you are sure you know what to do, you may go on with the rest of the page.

Sample A:
- Ⓐ theirfore
- Ⓑ therefour
- Ⓒ therefoer
- ⬤Ⓓ therefore

Sample B:
- Ⓔ cort
- Ⓕ court
- Ⓖ chort
- Ⓗ corte

1. Ⓐ pawse
   Ⓑ pause
   Ⓒ paus
   Ⓓ peuse

2. Ⓔ sord
   Ⓕ sorde
   Ⓖ sword
   Ⓗ swerd

3. Ⓐ walrus
   Ⓑ wallrus
   Ⓒ walris
   Ⓓ walres

4. Ⓔ worp
   Ⓕ warpe
   Ⓖ waurp
   Ⓗ warp

5. Ⓐ morne
   Ⓑ mourn
   Ⓒ mourne
   Ⓓ morrne

6. Ⓔ ignor
   Ⓕ ignawr
   Ⓖ ignore
   Ⓗ iggnor

7. Ⓐ aurght
   Ⓑ awght
   Ⓒ oght
   Ⓓ ought

8. Ⓔ ferk
   Ⓕ fawrk
   Ⓖ fork
   Ⓗ forke

9. Ⓐ laundry
   Ⓑ loundry
   Ⓒ lawndry
   Ⓓ lowndry

10. Ⓔ lywyer
    Ⓕ lawyer
    Ⓖ lawyr
    Ⓗ lawyur

11. Ⓐ sorte
    Ⓑ corte
    Ⓒ sert
    Ⓓ sort

12. Ⓔ faucet
    Ⓕ faucette
    Ⓖ fawcet
    Ⓗ foucette

13. Ⓐ fawsee
    Ⓑ forse
    Ⓒ foresee
    Ⓓ forsee

14. Ⓔ wadrobe
    Ⓕ wardrobe
    Ⓖ wardrob
    Ⓗ wordrobe

15. Ⓐ cawe
    Ⓑ cor
    Ⓒ core
    Ⓓ corre

16. Ⓔ wharf
    Ⓕ warf
    Ⓖ whorf
    Ⓗ worf

17. Ⓐ alminac
    Ⓑ almanac
    Ⓒ allmanac
    Ⓓ allmanak

18. Ⓔ risource
    Ⓕ resaurce
    Ⓖ resorce
    Ⓗ resource

19. Ⓐ thaughtless
    Ⓑ thoughtliss
    Ⓒ thoughtless
    Ⓓ thauthless

20. Ⓔ flowe
    Ⓕ flawe
    Ⓖ flaow
    Ⓗ flaw

Name_____ Date_____

Words with /är/ and /âr/

Pretest Directions

Fold back the paper along the dotted line. Use the blanks to write each word as it is read aloud. When you finish the test, unfold the paper. Use the list at the right to correct any spelling mistakes. Practice the words you missed for the Posttest.

To Parents

Here are the results of your child's weekly spelling Pretest. You can help your child study for the Posttest by following these simple steps for each word on the word list:

1. Read the word to your child.

2. Have your child write the word, saying each letter as it is written.

3. Say each letter of the word as your child checks the spelling.

4. If a mistake has been made, have your child read each letter of the correctly spelled word aloud, and then repeat steps 1–3.

1. _____	1. sharpen
2. _____	2. stared
3. _____	3. charm
4. _____	4. guard
5. _____	5. prairie
6. _____	6. flare
7. _____	7. canary
8. _____	8. garlic
9. _____	9. aircraft
10. _____	10. tar
11. _____	11. mare
12. _____	12. wary
13. _____	13. farewell
14. _____	14. librarian
15. _____	15. barbecue
16. _____	16. despair
17. _____	17. starch
18. _____	18. artificial
19. _____	19. carefree
20. _____	20. impaired

Challenge Words

_____ cut-out

_____ dented

_____ flurries

_____ frothing

_____ narrative

Words with /är/ and /âr/

Using the Word Study Steps

1. LOOK at the word
2. SAY the word aloud.
3. STUDY the letters in the word.
4. WRITE the word.
5. CHECK the word.

   Did you spell the word right?
   If not, go back to step 1.

Spelling Tip

Use words you know how to spell to help you spell new words.

sharp + en = sharpen

care + free = carefree

can + ary = canary

Find and Circle

Circle the spelling words in the puzzle.

a	i	r	c	r	a	f	t	w	i	n	s	t	a	r	e	d	o
s	t	a	r	c	h	w	a	r	y	m	h	g	a	r	l	i	c
f	l	a	r	e	g	u	a	r	d	b	a	r	b	e	c	u	e
m	a	r	e	e	f	a	r	e	w	e	l	l	m	e	t	a	r
l	i	b	r	a	r	i	a	n	o	i	m	p	a	i	r	e	d
c	h	a	r	m	t	r	a	l	t	p	r	a	i	r	i	e	v
h	o	n	s	h	a	r	p	e	n	c	a	n	a	r	y	i	l
g	a	r	t	i	f	i	c	i	a	l	f	i	t	y	x	v	m

To Parents or Helpers:

Using the Word Study Steps above as your child comes across any new spelling words will help him or her spell words effectively. Review the steps as you both go over this week's spelling words.

Go over the Spelling Tip with your child. Have him or her find other words that contain smaller words he or she knows how to spell.

Help your child complete the spelling activity.

Words with /är/ and /âr/

sharpen	prairie	aircraft	farewell	starch
stared	flare	tar	librarian	artificial
charm	canary	mare	barbecue	carefree
guard	garlic	wary	despair	impaired

Sort each spelling word according to the sound and spelling pattern to which it belongs.
Write the words with /är/ spelled as follows:

ar

1. _____   5. _____

2. _____   6. _____

3. _____   7. _____

4. _____   8. _____

Write the words with /âr/ spelled as follows:

air

9. _____

10. _____

11. _____

12. _____

ar

13. _____   17. _____

14. _____   18. _____

15. _____   19. _____

16. _____   20. _____

PRACTICE AND EXTEND

Words with /är/ and /âr/

sharpen	prairie	aircraft	farewell	starch
stared	flare	tar	librarian	artificial
charm	canary	mare	barbecue	carefree
guard	garlic	wary	despair	impaired

What Does It Mean?
Write the spelling word that matches each definition below.

1. looked at intently _____

2. female horse _____

3. protect _____

4. plane or jet _____

5. hopelessness _____

6. good-bye _____

7. man-made _____

8. damaged _____

9. untroubled _____

10. watchful _____

Complete each sentence below using a spelling word.

11. She gave birdseed to her pet _____.

12. They cooked hamburgers on the _____.

13. The school _____ helped him find the book.

14. You must _____ the scissors before you use them.

15. My friend has great _____.

16. The buffalo grazed on the _____.

17. They used a _____ to warn the drivers.

18. We ate _____ bread with our lasagne.

19. The hot sun softened the black _____ on the road.

20. His shirt looks very stiff from _____.

Words with /är/ and /âr/

Proofreading Activity
There are six spelling mistakes in the letter below. Circle the misspelled words.
Write the words correctly on the lines below.

Dear Grandma,

    In the school play I had to wear an artifishul red beard that was really itchy.
It also impared my speech. I tried my best to be a great actor. I even asked
the school libarian to help me find a book about acting. The book said to gard
against overacting. That means you should be wairy of waving around your
arms too much. Anyway, the play was a great success. When it was over,
the little kids in school staired at me as if I really were Robert De Niro.

                                        Love,
                                        Robert

1. _____   3. _____   5. _____

2. _____   4. _____   6. _____

Writing Activity
What kind of play would you like to act in? Write about the role you would like to have
in a school play. Use four spelling words in your writing.

_____

_____

_____

_____

Words with /är/and /âr/

Look at the words in each set below. One word in each set is spelled correctly. Use a pencil to fill in the circle next to the correct word. Before you begin, look at the sample sets of words. Sample A has been done for you. Do Sample B by yourself. When you are sure you know what to do, you may go on with the rest of the page.

Sample A:

- (A) repare
- (B) repear
- (C) repayr
- (D) **repair**

Sample B:

- (E) chartt
- (F) charrt
- (G) chart
- (H) charte

1.
- (A) shairpen
- (B) sherpen
- (C) sharpen
- (D) sharpin

6.
- (E) flaire
- (F) flear
- (G) flare
- (H) flayre

11.
- (A) mer
- (B) mayr
- (C) mair
- (D) mare

16.
- (E) dispair
- (F) despare
- (G) despair
- (H) despayr

2.
- (E) staired
- (F) stared
- (G) stayrd
- (H) stayred

7.
- (A) cunary
- (B) canary
- (C) cannary
- (D) canery

12.
- (E) waree
- (F) wary
- (G) wairy
- (H) waire

17.
- (A) stach
- (B) statch
- (C) startch
- (D) starch

3.
- (A) charm
- (B) cherm
- (C) churm
- (D) charem

8.
- (E) galic
- (F) garlic
- (G) garlick
- (H) gaurlic

13.
- (A) farwel
- (B) farewill
- (C) farewell
- (D) fairwel

18.
- (E) artificial
- (F) artefishial
- (G) artuficial
- (H) artifisal

4.
- (E) gard
- (F) gaurd
- (G) guard
- (H) gald

9.
- (A) aircraft
- (B) arecraft
- (C) aircreft
- (D) aircrafte

14.
- (E) librarian
- (F) libarian
- (G) liberrian
- (H) librairian

19.
- (A) carfree
- (B) carefree
- (C) cairfree
- (D) carefre

5.
- (A) prairy
- (B) prayry
- (C) prayrie
- (D) prairie

10.
- (E) ter
- (F) tare
- (G) tar
- (H) taur

15.
- (A) barrbequ
- (B) barbecue
- (C) baubecue
- (D) barbekew

20.
- (E) empaired
- (F) impared
- (G) impaired
- (H) umpaired

Words with /îr/ and /ûr/

Pretest Directions

Fold back the paper along the dotted line. Use the blanks to write each word as it is read aloud. When you finish the test, unfold the paper. Use the list at the right to correct any spelling mistakes. Practice the words you missed for the Posttest.

To Parents

Here are the results of your child's weekly spelling Pretest. You can help your child study for the Posttest by following these simple steps for each word on the word list:

1. Read the word to your child.

2. Have your child write the word, saying each letter as it is written.

3. Say each letter of the word as your child checks the spelling.

4. If a mistake has been made, have your child read each letter of the correctly spelled word aloud, and then repeat steps 1–3.

#		#	Word
1.	_____	1.	peer
2.	_____	2.	servants
3.	_____	3.	furnace
4.	_____	4.	pearl
5.	_____	5.	pierce
6.	_____	6.	interfere
7.	_____	7.	emergency
8.	_____	8.	fierce
9.	_____	9.	earnest
10.	_____	10.	journal
11.	_____	11.	pioneer
12.	_____	12.	personal
13.	_____	13.	urgent
14.	_____	14.	rehearse
15.	_____	15.	courtesy
16.	_____	16.	pier
17.	_____	17.	cashmere
18.	_____	18.	nourish
19.	_____	19.	sphere
20.	_____	20.	burnt

Challenge Words

_____ abide

_____ acceptable

_____ boyhood

_____ famine

_____ wares

Name_____ Date_____

Words with /îr/ and /ûr/

Using the Word Study Steps

1. LOOK at the word.
2. SAY the word aloud.
3. STUDY the letters in the word.
4. WRITE the word.
5. CHECK the word.

   Did you spell the word right?
   If not, go back to step 1.

Spelling Tip

Look for word chunks or smaller words that help you remember the spelling of the word. For example:

fur + nace = furnace

earn + est = earnest

can + ary = canary

What's Missing?

Fill in the missing letters in the spaces below to form spelling words.

1. p _____ r
2. s _____ vants
3. f _____ nace
4. p _____ rl
5. p _____ rce
6. interf _____
7. em _____ gency
8. f _____ rce
9. _____ rnest
10. j _____ rnal
11. pion _____ r
12. p _____ sonal
13. _____ gent
14. reh _____ rse
15. c _____ rtesy
16. p _____ r
17. cashm _____
18. n _____ rish
19. sph _____
20. b _____ nt

To Parents or Helpers:

Using the Word Study Steps above as your child comes across any new words will help him or her spell words effectively. Review the steps as you both go over this week's spelling words.

Go over the Spelling Tip with your child. Ask him or her to find other words that are made up of smaller words or word chunks that he or she knows.

Help your child complete the spelling activity by filling in the missing letters.

Words with /îr/ and /ûr/

peer	pierce	earnest	urgent	cashmere
servants	interfere	journal	rehearse	nourish
furnace	emergency	pioneer	courtesy	sphere
pearl	fierce	personal	pier	burnt

Sort each spelling word according to the sound and spelling pattern to which it belongs.
Write the words with /îr/ spelled as follows:

ere

1. _____

2. _____

3. _____

eer

4. _____

5. _____

ier

6. _____

7. _____

8. _____

Write the words with /ûr/ spelled as follows:

ur

9. _____

10. _____

11. _____

our

12. _____

13. _____

14. _____

er

15. _____

16. _____

17. _____

ear

18. _____

19. _____

20. _____

Words with /îr/ and /ûr/

peer	pierce	earnest	urgent	cashmere
servants	interfere	journal	rehearse	nourish
furnace	emergency	pioneer	courtesy	sphere
pearl	fierce	personal	pier	burnt

Finish the Sentence

Write the spelling word that best completes each sentence below.

1. He responded immediately to the _____ message.

2. This round orange has the shape of a perfect _____.

3. My aunt bought me a _____ sweater for my birthday.

4. The king and queen had many _____ in the palace.

5. The _____ toast tasted terrible.

6. The _____ in our house burns heating oil.

7. She received a _____ necklace on her wedding anniversary.

8. The _____ family traveled west in a covered wagon.

Word Meanings: Synonyms

Write the spelling word that has the same meaning as each word below.

9. equal _____   15. crisis _____

10. politeness _____   16. sincere _____

11. stab _____   17. dock _____

12. meddle _____   18. savage _____

13. private _____   19. diary _____

14. feed _____   20. practice _____

80

Challenge Extension: Write a short story using all of the Challenge Words.

Grade 6/Unit 3
The Singing Man | /20

Words with /îr/ and /ûr/

Proofreading Activity

There are six spelling mistakes in the paragraph below. Circle the misspelled words. Write the words correctly on the lines below.

This is what Banzar told the people of his village:

"The pain I felt when I left you so long ago would peerce my heart. But I had to follow my persinal dream of making music. Then I met Sholo. He was a musician without pere. I was very ernest in my music studies with Sholo. Together we would reherse songs for many hours every day. I hope my music will nurish your soul. I am so glad to be back among you, the people I love and care about."

1. _____ 3. _____ 5. _____

2. _____ 4. _____ 6. _____

Writing Activity

What personal dream do you have? Write about what you dream about doing when you are grown. Use four spelling words in your writing.

_____

_____

_____

_____

Words with /îr/ and /ûr/

Look at the words in each set below. One word in each set is spelled correctly. Use a pencil to fill in the circle next to the correct word. Before you begin, look at the sample sets of words. Sample A has been done for you. Do Sample B by yourself. When you are sure you know what to do, you may go on with the rest of the page.

Sample A:
- (A) burnning
- (B) bourning
- (C) burning
- (D) berning

Sample B:
- (E) steer
- (F) stear
- (G) stier
- (H) stere

1.
- (A) per
- (B) peer
- (C) pere
- (D) peere

2.
- (E) servants
- (F) servints
- (G) survants
- (H) servents

3.
- (A) funace
- (B) fernice
- (C) furnace
- (D) furnece

4.
- (E) pourl
- (F) perle
- (G) perl
- (H) pearl

5.
- (A) peerce
- (B) pierce
- (C) pierse
- (D) peirce

6.
- (E) interfere
- (F) innerfer
- (G) interfer
- (H) intufere

7.
- (A) emurguncy
- (B) emerjincy
- (C) emergency
- (D) emurgensy

8.
- (E) feerce
- (F) fierce
- (G) fearce
- (H) fierse

9.
- (A) ernest
- (B) urnest
- (C) earnist
- (D) earnest

10.
- (E) gournal
- (F) jurnal
- (G) journal
- (H) journul

11.
- (A) pieneer
- (B) piuneer
- (C) pionere
- (D) pioneer

12.
- (E) personal
- (F) persinal
- (G) pursonal
- (H) parsonal

13.
- (A) uhrgent
- (B) urgent
- (C) urgint
- (D) urrgent

14.
- (E) reherse
- (F) rehears
- (G) rehearse
- (H) rihearse

15.
- (A) courtesy
- (B) curtesy
- (C) courtisy
- (D) curtisy

16.
- (E) pere
- (F) peir
- (G) peere
- (H) pier

17.
- (A) cassmere
- (B) cashmere
- (C) cashmeer
- (D) cashumere

18.
- (E) nourish
- (F) nurish
- (G) norish
- (H) nourrish

19.
- (A) sfere
- (B) spher
- (C) sphere
- (D) shpere

20.
- (E) burnet
- (F) burnt
- (G) bernt
- (H) beurnt

Adding -ed and -ing

Pretest Directions

Fold back the paper along the dotted line. Use the blanks to write each word as it is read aloud. When you finish the test, unfold the paper. Use the list at the right to correct any spelling mistakes. Practice the words you missed for the Posttest.

To Parents

Here are the results of your child's weekly spelling Pretest. You can help your child study for the Posttest by following these simple steps for each word on the word list:

1. Read the word to your child.

2. Have your child write the word, saying each letter as it is written.

3. Say each letter of the word as your child checks the spelling.

4. If a mistake has been made, have your child read each letter of the correctly spelled word aloud, and then repeat steps 1–3.

1. _____	1. worried
2. _____	2. preferred
3. _____	3. equaled
4. _____	4. influencing
5. _____	5. observed
6. _____	6. uncovered
7. _____	7. preserved
8. _____	8. dignified
9. _____	9. identified
10. _____	10. permitting
11. _____	11. chiseled
12. _____	12. transferred
13. _____	13. illustrating
14. _____	14. allied
15. _____	15. reclining
16. _____	16. recurring
17. _____	17. advancing
18. _____	18. committed
19. _____	19. anticipating
20. _____	20. implied

Challenge Words

_____   engrave

_____   hibernate

_____   honeycombed

_____   sculpting

_____   scaffold

Name_____ Date_____

Adding *-ed* and *-ing*

Using the Word Study Steps

1. LOOK at the word.
2. SAY the word aloud.
3. STUDY the letters in the word.
4. WRITE the word.
5. CHECK the word.

   Did you spell the word right?
   If not, go back to step 1.

Spelling Tip

When words end in silent *e*, drop the *e* when adding *-ed* or *-ing*.

observ**e** + **ed** = observed
influenc**e** + **ing** = influencing

Related Words

Write the spelling word which is related to the words below.

1. worry _____
2. prefer _____
3. equal _____
4. influence _____
5. observe _____
6. uncover _____
7. preserve _____
8. dignify _____
9. identify _____
10. permit _____

11. chisel _____
12. transfer _____
13. illustrate _____
14. ally _____
15. recline _____
16. recur _____
17. advance _____
18. commit _____
19. anticipate _____
20. imply _____

To Parents or Helpers:

Using the Word Study Steps above as your child comes across any new words will help him or her spell words effectively. Review the steps as you both go over this week's spelling words.

Review the Spelling Tip with your child. Ask your child to find other spelling words that follow that rule.

Help your child complete the spelling activity by finding the related words.

Adding *-ed* and *-ing*

worried	observed	identified	illustrating	advancing
preferred	uncovered	permitting	allied	committed
equaled	preserved	chiseled	reclining	anticipating
influencing	dignified	transferred	recurring	implied

Sort the spelling words according to how each changes when adding *-ed* or *-ing*.
Write the words as follows:

Drop the final *e*

1. _____

2. _____

3. _____

4. _____

5. _____

6. _____

7. _____

Do not double the final consonant

8. _____

9. _____

10. _____

Double the final consonant

11. _____

12. _____

13. _____

14. _____

15. _____

Change *y* to *i*

16. _____

17. _____

18. _____

19. _____

20. _____

Adding -ed and -ing

worried	observed	identified	illustrating	advancing
preferred	uncovered	permitting	allied	committed
equaled	preserved	chiseled	reclining	anticipating
influencing	dignified	transferred	recurring	implied

Word Meaning: Synonyms

Write the spelling word that has the same meaning as the words below.

1. expecting _____

2. affecting _____

3. noticed _____

4. saved _____

5. named _____

6. moved _____

7. allowing _____

8. meant _____

9. anxious _____

10. repeating _____

11. united _____

12. honored _____

Complete each sentence below with a spelling word.

13. He was _____ on the couch with his feet up.

14. The attacking army was _____ on the enemy fort.

15. She _____ tea to coffee.

16. He _____ the dish before he put it in the oven.

17. The boy _____ his name into the tree trunk with a knife.

18. This is a picture _____ how a car engine works.

19. My speed in the race _____ that of the fastest runner.

20. They were _____ to the politician's campaign.

Challenge Extension: Have students write fill-in sentences for each Challenge Word. Then have each student exchange sentences with a partner and see how many the other student can correctly fill in.

Grade 6/Unit 3
Painters of the Caves

20

Adding *-ed* and *-ing*

Proofreading Activity
There are six spelling mistakes in the paragraph below. Circle the misspelled words. Write the words correctly on the lines below.

The cave explorers were not worryed about going down into the deep cave. They observeed that the walls of the cave contained well perserved pictures of animals. Perhaps these were pictures illustrateing the ancient people's hunt for food. Perhaps the pictures implyed that ancient people thought the animals had magical powers. The cave explorers are commited to protecting these ancient cave paintings for all people and for the future.

1. _____ 3. _____ 5. _____

2. _____ 4. _____ 6. _____

Writing Activity
Write your ideas about why ancient people made cave paintings. Use four spelling words in your writing.

_____
_____
_____
_____

Adding *-ed* and *-ing*

Look at the words in each set below. One word in each set is spelled correctly. Use a pencil to fill in the circle next to the correct word. Before you begin, look at the sample sets of words. Sample A has been done for you. Do Sample B by yourself. When you are sure you know what to do, you may go on with the rest of the page.

Sample A:
- Ⓐ occurring
- Ⓑ occuring
- Ⓒ occurying
- Ⓓ ocurring

Sample B:
- Ⓔ cryed
- Ⓕ criyed
- Ⓖ cryied
- Ⓗ cried

1. Ⓐ worryed
   Ⓑ worried
   Ⓒ worred
   Ⓓ woried

2. Ⓔ preferred
   Ⓕ prefered
   Ⓖ preffered
   Ⓗ preferd

3. Ⓐ equald
   Ⓑ eqaled
   Ⓒ ekwaled
   Ⓓ equaled

4. Ⓔ infloincing
   Ⓕ influincing
   Ⓖ influencing
   Ⓗ influenceing

5. Ⓐ ubserved
   Ⓑ observed
   Ⓒ obzerved
   Ⓓ observeed

6. Ⓔ uncovered
   Ⓕ uncovereed
   Ⓖ uncoverd
   Ⓗ uncoffered

7. Ⓐ presserved
   Ⓑ preservd
   Ⓒ preserved
   Ⓓ preserveed

8. Ⓔ dijnified
   Ⓕ dignified
   Ⓖ dignufied
   Ⓗ dignifyed

9. Ⓐ identifyed
   Ⓑ identufyed
   Ⓒ identified
   Ⓓ identyfied

10. Ⓔ permiting
    Ⓕ permitting
    Ⓖ permting
    Ⓗ purmiting

11. Ⓐ chiseled
    Ⓑ chizeled
    Ⓒ chiselled
    Ⓓ chisseled

12. Ⓔ transfered
    Ⓕ transffered
    Ⓖ transferred
    Ⓗ transferd

13. Ⓐ ilustrateing
    Ⓑ ilustrating
    Ⓒ illustrateing
    Ⓓ illustrating

14. Ⓔ allyed
    Ⓕ allied
    Ⓖ alyed
    Ⓗ alied

15. Ⓐ reclineing
    Ⓑ reklining
    Ⓒ reclining
    Ⓓ reclineing

16. Ⓔ recurring
    Ⓕ recuring
    Ⓖ reccuring
    Ⓗ reccurring

17. Ⓐ advanceing
    Ⓑ advancing
    Ⓒ advansing
    Ⓓ advanssing

18. Ⓔ comited
    Ⓕ commited
    Ⓖ committed
    Ⓗ comitted

19. Ⓐ anticipating
    Ⓑ anticipateing
    Ⓒ antisipateing
    Ⓓ anticipatting

20. Ⓔ implyed
    Ⓕ impllied
    Ⓖ implied
    Ⓗ implyd

Words from Music

Pretest Directions

Fold back the paper along the dotted line. Use the blanks to write each word as it is read aloud. When you finish the test, unfold the paper. Use the list at the right to correct any spelling mistakes. Practice the words you missed for the Posttest.

To Parents

Here are the results of your child's weekly spelling Pretest. You can help your child study for the Posttest by following these simple steps for each word on the word list:

1. Read the word to your child.

2. Have your child write the word, saying each letter as it is written.

3. Say each letter of the word as your child checks the spelling.

4. If a mistake has been made, have your child read each letter of the correctly spelled word aloud, and then repeat steps 1–3.

1.	_____	1. musical
2.	_____	2. major
3.	_____	3. modern
4.	_____	4. guitar
5.	_____	5. concert
6.	_____	6. soprano
7.	_____	7. harmony
8.	_____	8. melody
9.	_____	9. accompany
10.	_____	10. percussion
11.	_____	11. opera
12.	_____	12. cymbal
13.	_____	13. accordion
14.	_____	14. lyrics
15.	_____	15. crescendo
16.	_____	16. alto
17.	_____	17. duration
18.	_____	18. dynamics
19.	_____	19. octave
20.	_____	20. allegro

Challenge Words

_____ brute

_____ complex

_____ controversy

_____ perceptions

_____ punctured

Name_____ Date_____

Words from Music

Using the Word Study Steps

1. LOOK at the word
2. SAY the word aloud.
3. STUDY the letters in the word.
4. WRITE the word.
5. CHECK the word.

   Did you spell the word right?
   If not, go back to step 1.

Spelling Tip

Look for word chunks or smaller words that help you remember the spelling of larger words.

gui **tar**
harm ony
ac **company**

Find and Circle

Find and circle the spelling words hidden in each set of letters.

1. s t a m u s i c a l y t i n o c a l
2. m a j o r i v e n t k l f g h k a m
3. d o m r e n s m o d e r n s t l o
4. h a g u i t a r t r n i m b e r m i
5. r s o t h i e v e d c o n c e r t y
6. t h a u m h a r m o n y s u t e
7. s t e n m e l o d y e n u s t y a
8. r a c c o m p a n y e r i a n o l
9. s p u r p e l p e r c u s s i o n y
10. r o e o p e r a r e o r p p t s n o

To Parents or Helpers:

Using the Word Study Steps above as your child comes across any new words will help him or her spell words effectively. Review the steps as you both go over this week's spelling words.

Ask your child to find word chunks or smaller words in this week's spelling words. Help your child complete the spelling activity.

Words from Music

musical	concert	accompany	accordion	duration
major	soprano	percussion	lyrics	dynamics
modern	harmony	opera	crescendo	octave
guitar	melody	cymbal	alto	allegro

Say each spelling word aloud and listen for the accent. Then write the words which fit the following patterns:

Accented first syllable

1. _____
2. _____
3. _____
4. _____
5. _____
6. _____
7. _____
8. _____
9. _____
10. _____
11. _____

Accented second syllable

12. _____
13. _____
14. _____
15. _____
16. _____
17. _____
18. _____
19. _____
20. _____

Find the Word

Write the spelling word that contains each of the following smaller words

21. accord _____
22. ran _____
23. company _____
24. harm _____
25. leg _____

Words from Music

musical	concert	accompany	accordion	duration
major	soprano	percussion	lyrics	dynamics
modern	harmony	opera	crescendo	octave
guitar	melody	cymbal	alto	allegro

Part of a Group
Read the heading for each group of words. Then add the spelling word that belongs in each group.

1. Stringed Instruments: violin, banjo, _____

2. Rhythm Instruments: drum, triangle, _____

3. Parts of a Song: tune, refrain, _____

4. Instruments with Keys: piano, keyboard, _____

5. Kinds of Music: rock and roll, country, _____

Definitions
Write the spelling word which matches each definition below.

6. gradual increase _____   **10.** tune _____

7. lively _____   **11.** low female voice _____

8. highest female voice _____   **12.** span of notes _____

9. structure of chords _____

Sentence Completions

13. The singer in the _____ has a beautiful voice.

14. On Saturday, I'm going to a _____ to see my favorite band.

15. Is that song in a minor key or in a _____ key?

16. Which pianist will _____ the singer?

17. A rest in music is the _____ of silence between notes.

18. The radio station plays only the most _____ hits.

Challenge Extension: Write one sentence for each Challenge Word.

Words from Music

Proofreading Activity
There are six spelling mistakes in the paragraph below. Circle the misspelled words. Write the words correctly on the lines below.

The Neanderthals sat around the fire in the cave. After a while, a woman began humming a meloddy. Soon another woman joined in, singing in harminy with the first. A man added perkussion, pounding rhythmically on a flat rock. Then everyone began to acompany the music by clapping hands or humming. The Neanderthals were in some way musicel, like modurn people.

1. _____ 3. _____ 5. _____

2. _____ 4. _____ 6. _____

Writing Activity
Pretend you are a musician in a band. What instrument would you play? Write about your band. Use four spelling words in your writing.

_____

_____

_____

_____

10 Grade 6/Unit 3
Is This Ancient Bone the
World's First Flute?

93

Words from Music

Look at the words in each set below. One word in each set is spelled correctly. Use a pencil to fill in the circle next to the correct word. Before you begin, look at the sample sets of words. Sample A has been done for you. Do Sample B by yourself. When you are sure you know what to do, you may go on with the rest of the page.

Sample A:
- Ⓐ drumer
- Ⓑ drummir
- ⬤ drummer
- Ⓓ drumur

Sample B:
- Ⓔ pyano
- Ⓕ pianot
- Ⓖ peano
- Ⓗ piano

1.
- Ⓐ musickal
- Ⓑ myusical
- Ⓒ mosical
- Ⓓ musical

2.
- Ⓔ madjer
- Ⓕ major
- Ⓖ magor
- Ⓗ madjor

3.
- Ⓐ modirn
- Ⓑ madern
- Ⓒ modern
- Ⓓ moden

4.
- Ⓔ guitar
- Ⓕ gitar
- Ⓖ guhtar
- Ⓗ guiter

5.
- Ⓐ consert
- Ⓑ concert
- Ⓒ concerte
- Ⓓ consurt

6.
- Ⓔ spranoh
- Ⓕ soprenoh
- Ⓖ soprano
- Ⓗ sooprano

7.
- Ⓐ harmonee
- Ⓑ harmonie
- Ⓒ harmeny
- Ⓓ harmony

8.
- Ⓔ melodie
- Ⓕ melody
- Ⓖ milody
- Ⓗ meludy

9.
- Ⓐ accompany
- Ⓑ acompany
- Ⓒ ackompany
- Ⓓ accompeny

10.
- Ⓔ perkussion
- Ⓕ percussion
- Ⓖ purcussion
- Ⓗ percustion

11.
- Ⓐ apera
- Ⓑ oppera
- Ⓒ opera
- Ⓓ oppero

12.
- Ⓔ cymbal
- Ⓕ symbal
- Ⓖ cimbal
- Ⓗ cymbul

13.
- Ⓐ acordion
- Ⓑ accordion
- Ⓒ accordian
- Ⓓ ackordian

14.
- Ⓔ lirics
- Ⓕ liriks
- Ⓖ lyricks
- Ⓗ lyrics

15.
- Ⓐ cressendo
- Ⓑ criscendo
- Ⓒ crescendo
- Ⓓ crussendo

16.
- Ⓔ altoo
- Ⓕ alto
- Ⓖ allto
- Ⓗ altow

17.
- Ⓐ duration
- Ⓑ dooration
- Ⓒ durasion
- Ⓓ deration

18.
- Ⓔ dinamics
- Ⓕ dienamics
- Ⓖ dyenamics
- Ⓗ dynamics

19.
- Ⓐ octiv
- Ⓑ octave
- Ⓒ octav
- Ⓓ ocktave

20.
- Ⓔ alegro
- Ⓕ allegrow
- Ⓖ allegro
- Ⓗ aleggro

Grade 6/Unit 3 Review Test

Read each sentence. If an underlined word is spelled wrong, fill in the circle that goes with that word. If no word is spelled wrong, fill in the circle below NONE.

Read Sample A and do Sample B.

A. They were <u>wurried</u> about <u>illustrating</u> the <u>volume</u>.
        A   B   C

NONE
A. Ⓐ Ⓑ Ⓒ Ⓓ

B. He <u>uncovered</u> the <u>accordion</u> and played one <u>octiv</u>.
     E   F   G

NONE
B. Ⓔ Ⓕ Ⓖ Ⓗ

1. You <u>ought</u> to wash the <u>casmere</u> sweater under the <u>faucet</u>.
      A   B   C

NONE
1. Ⓐ Ⓑ Ⓒ Ⓓ

2. The <u>almanack</u> <u>implied</u> that it would rain on the <u>prairie</u>.
     E   F   G

NONE
2. Ⓔ Ⓕ Ⓖ Ⓗ

3. The <u>suprano</u> could not sing the <u>recurring</u> <u>melody</u>.
      A   B   C

NONE
3. Ⓐ Ⓑ Ⓒ Ⓓ

4. Did you <u>forsee</u> her <u>carefree</u> attitude at the <u>barbecue</u>?
        E   F   G

NONE
4. Ⓔ Ⓕ Ⓖ Ⓗ

5. A <u>wardrobe</u> <u>ought</u> not to be made of <u>artificial</u> wood.
    A   B   C

NONE
5. Ⓐ Ⓑ Ⓒ Ⓓ

6. The <u>earnest</u> sculptor <u>chiseled</u> the <u>wardrobe</u>.
     E   F   G

NONE
6. Ⓔ Ⓕ Ⓖ Ⓗ

7. We <u>foresee</u> a <u>cairfree</u> vacation on the <u>prairie</u>.
     A   B   C

NONE
7. Ⓐ Ⓑ Ⓒ Ⓓ

8. The <u>creshendo</u> had a <u>recurring</u> clanging of the <u>cymbal</u>.
     E   F   G

NONE
8. Ⓔ Ⓕ Ⓖ Ⓗ

9. The <u>carefree</u> <u>pioneer</u> <u>chizeled</u> his name in the tree.
     A   B   C

NONE
9. Ⓐ Ⓑ Ⓒ Ⓓ

10. The <u>soprano</u> was <u>dignified</u> and treated us with <u>curtesy</u>.
      E   F   G

NONE
10. Ⓔ Ⓕ Ⓖ Ⓗ

Go on →

Grade 6/Unit 3 Review Test

11. You <u>ought</u> not use <u>artificial</u> <u>barbekew</u> sauce. 11. Ⓐ Ⓑ Ⓒ Ⓓ (NONE)
       A   B   C

12. It is <u>urgent</u> that we fix the <u>recurring</u> leak in the <u>faucit</u>. 12. Ⓔ Ⓕ Ⓖ Ⓗ (NONE)
      E   F   G

13. The <u>recurring</u> <u>melody</u> was <u>influancing</u> us. 13. Ⓐ Ⓑ Ⓒ Ⓓ (NONE)
     A   B   C

14. The <u>pioneer</u> <u>implied</u> that he had an <u>ergent</u> message. 14. Ⓔ Ⓕ Ⓖ Ⓗ (NONE)
     E   F   G

15. The <u>canary</u> sang an <u>earnest</u> <u>mellody</u>. 15. Ⓐ Ⓑ Ⓒ Ⓓ (NONE)
     A   B   C

16. The <u>diggnified</u> man <u>implied</u> that we lacked <u>courtesy</u>. 16. Ⓔ Ⓕ Ⓖ Ⓗ (NONE)
     E   F   G

17. The <u>pioneer</u> brought a <u>canary</u> to the <u>prayrie</u>. 17. Ⓐ Ⓑ Ⓒ Ⓓ (NONE)
     A   B   C

18. The <u>soprano</u> sang a <u>melody</u> in <u>harmony</u>. 18. Ⓔ Ⓕ Ⓖ Ⓗ (NONE)
     E   F   G

19. The <u>almanac</u> <u>aught</u> to help you <u>foresee</u> the weather. 19. Ⓐ Ⓑ Ⓒ Ⓓ (NONE)
     A   B   C

20. My <u>wardrobe</u> has both <u>cashmeer</u> and <u>artificial</u> wool. 20. Ⓔ Ⓕ Ⓖ Ⓗ (NONE)
     E   F   G

21. Have the <u>courtesy</u> to listen to the <u>harmonie</u> and <u>crescendo</u>. 21. Ⓐ Ⓑ Ⓒ Ⓓ (NONE)
        A   B   C

22. Whoever wrote the <u>almanac</u> can <u>foresee</u> <u>recuring</u> rains. 22. Ⓔ Ⓕ Ⓖ Ⓗ (NONE)
        E   F   G

23. The <u>symbal</u> was <u>influencing</u> the <u>crescendo</u>. 23. Ⓐ Ⓑ Ⓒ Ⓓ (NONE)
     A   B   C

24. The <u>soprano</u> looked <u>ernest</u> and <u>dignified</u>. 24. Ⓔ Ⓕ Ⓖ Ⓗ (NONE)
     E   F   G

25. I was <u>influencing</u> the <u>pionere</u> at the <u>barbecue</u>. 25. Ⓐ Ⓑ Ⓒ Ⓓ (NONE)
     A   B   C

Words with /sh/, /ch/, and /zh/

Pretest Directions

Fold back the paper along the dotted line. Use the blanks to write each word as it is read aloud. When you finish the test, unfold the paper. Use the list at the right to correct any spelling mistakes. Practice the words you missed for the Posttest.

To Parents

Here are the results of your child's weekly spelling Pretest. You can help your child study for the Posttest by following these simple steps for each word on the word list:

1. Read the word to your child.

2. Have your child write the word, saying each letter as it is written.

3. Say each letter of the word as your child checks the spelling.

4. If a mistake has been made, have your child read each letter of the correctly spelled word aloud, and then repeat steps 1–3.

#		#	Word
1.	_____	1.	chestnut
2.	_____	2.	shrunken
3.	_____	3.	treasure
4.	_____	4.	mixture
5.	_____	5.	foundations
6.	_____	6.	decision
7.	_____	7.	officials
8.	_____	8.	tissue
9.	_____	9.	leisure
10.	_____	10.	vision
11.	_____	11.	lurch
12.	_____	12.	vulture
13.	_____	13.	partial
14.	_____	14.	glacier
15.	_____	15.	enclosure
16.	_____	16.	charity
17.	_____	17.	session
18.	_____	18.	establish
19.	_____	19.	miniature
20.	_____	20.	superstitious

Challenge Words

_____ bazaars

_____ coffins

_____ dramatically

_____ pharaoh

_____ tomb

Name_____ Date_____ **Spelling**

Words with /sh/, /ch/, and /zh/

Using the Word Study Steps

1. LOOK at the word
2. SAY the word aloud.
3. STUDY the letters in the word.
4. WRITE the word.
5. CHECK the word.

   Did you spell the word right?
   If not, go back to step 1.

Spelling Tip

When followed by a vowel, *ti* and *ci* often spell the /*sh*/ sound, except at the beginning of a word.

founda<u>ti</u>ons

gla<u>ci</u>er

Word Scramble

Unscramble each set of letters to make a spelling word.

1. tayirhc _____
2. ernutaiim _____
3. niosiv _____
4. renusloce _____
5. nsoises _____
6. reaiclg _____
7. arlitap _____
8. slfaicifo _____
9. hssiblate _____
10. tiuesoitsrups _____

11. reuutlv _____
12. nsoiiced _____
13. riesuel _____
14. irxtuem _____
15. teuntsch _____
16. nehknrus _____
17. esuist _____
18. soitdannufo _____
19. hclur _____
20. eruaerst _____

To Parents or Helpers:

Using the Word Study Steps above as your child comes across any new words will help him or her learn to spell words effectively. Review the steps as you both go over this week's spelling words.

Go over the Spelling Tip with your child. Ask your child if he or she can find one spelling word with the *ti* spelling pattern, and one with the *ci* that have the /sh/ sound.

Help your child complete the word scramble.

Words with /sh/, /ch/, and /zh/

chestnut	foundations	leisure	partial	session
shrunken	decision	vision	glacier	establish
treasure	officials	lurch	enclosure	miniature
mixture	tissue	vulture	charity	superstitious

Sort each spelling word by finding the sound and spelling pattern to which it belongs. Write the word and draw a line under the letter or letters that spell its sound.

/sh/ spelled:

sh

1. _____

2. _____

ti

3. _____

4. _____

5. _____

ci

6. _____

7. _____

ss

8. _____

9. _____

/ch/ spelled:

ch

10. _____

11. _____

12. _____

t

13. _____

14. _____

15. _____

/zh/ spelled:

si

16. _____

17. _____

s

18. _____

19. _____

20. _____

Name_____ Date_____

Words with /sh/, /ch/, and /zh/

chestnut	foundations	leisure	partial	session
shrunken	decision	vision	glacier	establish
treasure	officials	lurch	enclosure	miniature
mixture	tissue	vulture	charity	superstitious

Complete each sentence with a spelling word.

1. A _____ of red and green makes brown.

2. The fence forms an _____ around the ranch.

3. We will find the hidden _____ on a deserted island.

4. The president and vice president are _____ at the bank.

5. I made the _____ to buy an umbrella.

6. The _____ for the homes must be laid first.

7. A sheet of thin _____ was wrapped around the box.

8. The huge _____ swooped down to eat the dead animal.

9. I collect clothing to give to a children's _____ every year.

10. It is _____ to think that a broken mirror brings bad luck.

11. You should first _____ your plans before carrying them out.

12. Please don't enter the courtroom now that it is in _____.

Definitions
Write the spelling word that best matches the definition.

13. large ice _____

14. incomplete _____

15. nut from a tree _____

16. made smaller _____

17. sight _____

18. very small _____

19. jerky move _____

20. free time _____

Challenge Extension: Have students create a fill-in
sentence for each Challenge Word, exchange papers
with partners, and complete each other's sentences.

Grade 6/Unit 4
Mummies, Tombs, and Treasures

20

Words with /sh/, /ch/, and /zh/

Proofreading Activity

There are six spelling mistakes in the paragraph below. Circle each misspelled word. Write the words correctly on the lines below.

Howard had a visun of finding an undisturbed tomb. A wealthy nobleman made a decician to fund his work. While digging under the foundacions of some huts, his workers found a tomb. Although robbers had stolen some of the miniachure items, the coffin was undisturbed. The coffin was full of treazure, but the mummy itself was blackened and shrunkin.

1. _____   3. _____   5. _____

2. _____   4. _____   6. _____

Writing Activity

Suppose Carter were keeping a journal of his experiences digging for the tomb. Write a journal entry he might have written. Use at least four spelling words.

_____

_____

_____

_____

Words with /sh/, /ch/, and /zh/

Look at the words in each set below. One word in each set is spelled correctly. Use a pencil to fill in the circle next to the correct word. Before you begin, look at the sample sets of words. Sample A has been done for you. Do Sample B by yourself. When you are sure you know what to do, you may go on with the rest of the page.

Sample A:
- Ⓐ vacashun
- Ⓑ vacashion
- ● vacation
- Ⓓ vacaton

Sample B:
- Ⓔ pictere
- Ⓕ picture
- Ⓖ pichure
- Ⓗ pictchure

1.
- Ⓐ tishue
- Ⓑ tishoo
- Ⓒ tissue
- Ⓓ tissoo

2.
- Ⓔ officals
- Ⓕ officials
- Ⓖ offishials
- Ⓗ offishals

3.
- Ⓐ leizure
- Ⓑ leazure
- Ⓒ leisure
- Ⓓ leasurr

4.
- Ⓔ decision
- Ⓕ decizion
- Ⓖ decisun
- Ⓗ decizun

5.
- Ⓐ foundashions
- Ⓑ foundashuns
- Ⓒ foundations
- Ⓓ foundatiuns

6.
- Ⓔ vission
- Ⓕ visson
- Ⓖ vision
- Ⓗ vison

7.
- Ⓐ mixture
- Ⓑ mixchure
- Ⓒ mixtchure
- Ⓓ mixtur

8.
- Ⓔ lurtch
- Ⓕ lurch
- Ⓖ lertch
- Ⓗ lerch

9.
- Ⓐ trezure
- Ⓑ treazure
- Ⓒ treasure
- Ⓓ tresure

10.
- Ⓔ vulchure
- Ⓕ vultchure
- Ⓖ vulture
- Ⓗ vultere

11.
- Ⓐ shrunken
- Ⓑ shrunkin
- Ⓒ srunken
- Ⓓ srunkin

12.
- Ⓔ parcial
- Ⓕ parshial
- Ⓖ partal
- Ⓗ partial

13.
- Ⓐ chesnut
- Ⓑ chestnut
- Ⓒ chistnut
- Ⓓ cheastnut

14.
- Ⓔ seshion
- Ⓕ sesion
- Ⓖ session
- Ⓗ sescion

15.
- Ⓐ chairity
- Ⓑ chairety
- Ⓒ charety
- Ⓓ charity

16.
- Ⓔ enclozure
- Ⓕ enclosure
- Ⓖ enclosere
- Ⓗ enclozere

17.
- Ⓐ miniature
- Ⓑ miniture
- Ⓒ minachure
- Ⓓ miniatchure

18.
- Ⓔ glatier
- Ⓕ glacier
- Ⓖ glassier
- Ⓗ glasher

19.
- Ⓐ supersticious
- Ⓑ superstishious
- Ⓒ superstitious
- Ⓓ superstishous

20.
- Ⓔ establiss
- Ⓕ establish
- Ⓖ astablish
- Ⓗ istablish

Words with /ər/, /əl/, and /ən/

Pretest Directions

Fold back the paper along the dotted line. Use the blanks to write each word as it is read aloud. When you finish the test, unfold the paper. Use the list at the right to correct any spelling mistakes. Practice the words you missed for the Posttest.

To Parents

Here are the results of your child's weekly spelling Pretest. You can help your child study for the Posttest by following these simple steps for each word on the word list:

1. Read the word to your child.

2. Have your child write the word, saying each letter as it is written.

3. Say each letter of the word as your child checks the spelling.

4. If a mistake has been made, have your child read each letter of the correctly spelled word aloud, and then repeat steps 1–3.

1. _____	1. underwater
2. _____	2. samples
3. _____	3. widen
4. _____	4. similar
5. _____	5. superior
6. _____	6. panel
7. _____	7. practical
8. _____	8. melon
9. _____	9. urban
10. _____	10. manner
11. _____	11. article
12. _____	12. mistaken
13. _____	13. jumbles
14. _____	14. cedar
15. _____	15. funnel
16. _____	16. fatal
17. _____	17. moral
18. _____	18. vapor
19. _____	19. unison
20. _____	20. tremor

Challenge Words

_____ accumulating

_____ environmental

_____ formation

_____ industrial

_____ submerged

Words with /ər/, /əl/, and /ən/

Using the Word Study Steps

1. LOOK at the word.
2. SAY the word aloud.
3. STUDY the letters in the word.
4. WRITE the word.
5. CHECK the word.

   Did you spell the word right?
   If not, go back to step 1.

Spelling Tip

The schwa /ə/ is a vowel sound. The spelling of the schwa sound always includes an *a, e, i, o,* or *u.*

ced<u>a</u>r   mann<u>e</u>r   penc<u>i</u>l

vap<u>o</u>r   circ<u>u</u>s

Alphabetical Order

List each spelling word in alphabetical order.

1. _____
2. _____
3. _____
4. _____
5. _____
6. _____
7. _____

8. _____
9. _____
10. _____
11. _____
12. _____
13. _____
14. _____

15. _____
16. _____
17. _____
18. _____
19. _____
20. _____

To Parents or Helpers:

Using the Word Study Steps above as your child comes across any new words will help him or her learn to spell words effectively. Review the steps as you both go over this week's spelling words.

Go over the Spelling Tip with your child. Have your child say the words aloud. Point out to him or her that the schwa is always spelled with an *a, e, i, o,* or *u.*

Help your child complete the alphabetical order activity.

Name_____ Date_____

Words with /ər/, /əl/, and /ən/

underwater	superior	urban	jumbles	moral
samples	panel	manner	cedar	vapor
widen	practical	article	funnel	unison
similar	melon	mistaken	fatal	tremor

Sort each spelling word by finding the sound and spelling pattern to which it belongs. Write the word and underline the letters that spell its vowel sound.

/ər/ spelled

er

1. _____

2. _____

ar

3. _____

4. _____

or

5. _____

6. _____

7. _____

/əl/ spelled

le

8. _____

9. _____

10. _____

el

11. _____

12. _____

al

13. _____

14. _____

15. _____

/ən/ spelled

en

16. _____

17. _____

on

18. _____

19. _____

an

20. _____

Words with /ər/, /əl/, and /ən/

underwater	superior	urban	jumbles	moral
samples	panel	manner	cedar	vapor
widen	practical	article	funnel	unison
similar	melon	mistaken	fatal	tremor

Complete each sentence below with a spelling word or words.

1. If we _____ the tunnel, we can crawl through it.

2. Did you read the _____ on space travel in the newspaper?

3. Pass out the muffin _____ for a taste test.

4 Our _____ of judges will make the final decision.

5. He used a very professional _____ when telling the problem.

6. Our basement contains _____ of odds and ends.

7. You can use a _____ to pour the milk into the container.

8. A _____ person cares about what is right and what is wrong.

Definitions
Write the spelling word that best matches the definition or synonym.

9. kind of fruit _____

10. about a city _____

11. wood _____

12. causing death _____

13. gas _____

14. together _____

15. below water _____

16. sensible _____

17. wrong _____

18. a shaking _____

19. better _____

20. alike _____

Challenge Extension: Have students use the Challenge Words in a paragraph about pollution.

Grade 6/Unit 4
Over the Top of the World 20

Words with /ər/, /əl/, and /ən/

Proofreading Activity

There are six spelling mistakes in the paragraph below. Circle each misspelled word.
Write the words correctly on the lines below.

The artikle, "Over the Top of the World," describes a journey across the frozen

arctic. One purpose of the trip was to collect snow sampels. One day a tremer

shook the ice and it cracked. In horror, people watched the crack widan. One of the

sled dogs almost fell through the crack into the ocean. A few minutes underwatar

could be fatel. Fortunately, his team managed to pull him to safety.

1. _____   3. _____   5. _____

2. _____   4. _____   6. _____

Writing Activity

In "Over the Top of the World," team members used a computer to send reports to
interested people all over the world. Write a report that they might have sent on one
of the days described in the article. Use at least four spelling words.

_____

_____

_____

_____

Words with /ər/, /əl/, and /ən/

Look at the words in each set below. One word in each set is spelled correctly. Use a pencil to fill in the circle next to the correct word. Before you begin, look at the sample sets of words. Sample A has been done for you. Do Sample B by yourself. When you are sure you know what to do, you may go on with the rest of the page.

Sample A:

- (A) bakir
- (B) bakar
- (C) baker
- (D) bakur

Sample B:

- (E) people
- (F) poeple
- (G) peopel
- (H) peapel

1. (A) ceder
(B) cedor
(C) cedar
(D) cedur

2. (E) sampels
(F) samples
(G) sampals
(H) sammples

3. (A) erban
(B) erbin
(C) urbin
(D) urban

4. (E) vapor
(F) vaper
(G) vapir
(H) vapar

5. (A) supearior
(B) supearier
(C) superior
(D) superier

6. (E) practicle
(F) practicel
(G) practical
(H) practicil

7. (A) jumbles
(B) jumbels
(C) jumbals
(D) jummbles

8. (E) undurwater
(F) underwatur
(G) underwater
(H) underwauter

9. (A) tremer
(B) tremar
(C) tremor
(D) tremmor

10. (E) widon
(F) widden
(G) widdon
(H) widen

11. (A) article
(B) articel
(C) artical
(D) artacle

12. (E) morel
(F) morrel
(G) morral
(H) moral

13. (A) similor
(B) similar
(C) similer
(D) simlar

14. (E) unisen
(F) unasen
(G) unison
(H) unisan

15. (A) panal
(B) panle
(C) pannel
(D) panel

16. (E) fatle
(F) fatal
(G) fatel
(H) fattal

17. (A) melon
(B) melen
(C) melan
(D) melin

18. (E) funnol
(F) funnel
(G) funle
(H) funnal

19. (A) mannar
(B) mannor
(C) manner
(D) mannir

20. (E) mistakon
(F) mistaken
(G) mistakan
(H) mistakin

Spelling Unstressed Syllables

Pretest Directions

Fold back the paper along the dotted line. Use the blanks to write each word as it is read aloud. When you finish the test, unfold the paper. Use the list at the right to correct any spelling mistakes. Practice the words you missed for the Posttest.

To Parents

Here are the results of your child's weekly spelling Pretest. You can help your child study for the Posttest by following these simple steps for each word on the word list:

1. Read the word to your child.

2. Have your child write the word, saying each letter as it is written.

3. Say each letter of the word as your child checks the spelling.

4. If a mistake has been made, have your child read each letter of the correctly spelled word aloud, and then repeat steps 1–3.

1. _____	1. suppose
2. _____	2. stubborn
3. _____	3. perhaps
4. _____	4. confess
5. _____	5. appeal
6. _____	6. album
7. _____	7. effort
8. _____	8. severe
9. _____	9. canvas
10. _____	10. ballot
11. _____	11. morsel
12. _____	12. standard
13. _____	13. applause
14. _____	14. nuisance
15. _____	15. judgment
16. _____	16. ponder
17. _____	17. suspend
18. _____	18. collide
19. _____	19. ballad
20. _____	20. random

Challenge Words

_____	appreciation
_____	cellophane
_____	explosions
_____	tollbooth
_____	triangles

Spelling Unstressed Syllables

Using the Word Study Steps

1. LOOK at the word
2. SAY the word aloud.
3. STUDY the letters in the word.
4. WRITE the word.
5. CHECK the word.

   Did you spell the word right?
   If not, go back to step 1.

Spelling Tip

An unstressed syllable is said with very little force. When the unstressed syllable includes a schwa /ə/, the sound is the same no matter whether spelled with an *a, e, i, o, or u.*

canv<u>a</u>s   mors<u>e</u>l   penc<u>i</u>l

ball<u>o</u>t   alb<u>u</u>m

Word Scramble

Unscramble each set of letters to make a spelling word.

1. taollb _____
2. rnobutsb _____
3. seppuso _____
4. nsedpsu _____
5. plapea _____
6. elosrm _____
7. trfeof _____
8. laadlb _____
9. asnvac _____
10. sparehp _____

11. netgjmdu _____
12. dmnaor _____
13. sefosnc _____
14. nsecauin _____
15. radntads _____
16. endrpo _____
17. umbla _____
18. diloelc _____
19. eeresv _____
20. asuelppa _____

To Parents or Helpers:

Using the Word Study Steps above as your child comes across any new words will help him or her learn to spell words effectively. Review the steps as you both go over this week's spelling words.

Go over the Spelling Tip with your child. Have your child say the five words aloud asking him or her to notice that the schwa sound is the same in each word.

Help your child complete the word scramble.

Spelling Unstressed Syllables

suppose	appeal	canvas	applause	suspend
stubborn	album	ballot	nuisance	collide
perhaps	effort	morsel	judgment	ballad
confess	severe	standard	ponder	random

Sort each spelling word by finding the spelling pattern to which it belongs. Write the word and underline the letter that spells the schwa (/ə/) sound.

Write the spelling words with /ə/

spelled:

a

1. _____
2. _____
3. _____
4. _____
5. _____
6. _____

o

7. _____
8. _____
9. _____
10. _____
11. _____
12. _____

e

13. _____
14. _____
15. _____
16. _____
17. _____

u

18. _____
19. _____
20. _____

Spelling Unstressed Syllables

suppose	appeal	canvas	applause	suspend
stubborn	album	ballot	nuisance	collide
perhaps	effort	morsel	judgment	ballad
confess	severe	standard	ponder	random

Complete each sentence with a spelling word.

1. If you get another ticket, they will _____ your license.

2. I keep the best photographs in my photo _____.

3. The cowboy made a _____ choice of three horses to ride.

4. You must fill out a _____ if you want to vote.

5. Is it too much of an _____ to carry those books?

6. The _____ little boy refused to take his nap.

7. That painting was made on a large _____.

8. Swimming in very cold water does not _____ to me.

9. The student needs to work up to the class _____.

Matched Pairs
Write the spelling word that is related in meaning to the words below.

10. clash _____

11. harsh _____

12. clapping _____

13. bit _____

14. decision _____

15. think _____

16. pest _____

17. maybe _____

18. imagine _____

19. song _____

20. admit _____

112

Challenge Extension: Have students look up each Challenge Word in the dictionary. Then have them write one sentence for each word.

Grade 6/Unit 4
The Phantom Tollbooth
20

Spelling Unstressed Syllables

Proofreading Activity

There are six spelling mistakes in the paragraph below. Circle each misspelled word. Write the words correctly on the lines below.

Sappose people paid no attention to time? Even the Clock admitted time can be a nuisence. People put so much effert into doing what time tells them to do. In the Doldrums, people did not do much with their time. They were not even allowed to think or pondor. The lifestyle did not appeel to everyone, though. A Watchdog issued sivere warnings about wasting time.

1. _____   3. _____   5. _____

2. _____   4. _____   6. _____

Writing Activity

Make up a short and funny story about wasting time. Use four spelling words.

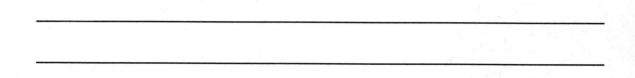

_____

_____

_____

_____

Spelling Unstressed Syllables

Look at the words in each set below. One word in each set is spelled correctly. Use a pencil to fill in the circle next to the correct word. Before you begin, look at the sample sets of words. Sample A has been done for you. Do Sample B by yourself. When you are sure you know what to do, you may go on with the rest of the page.

Sample A:
- Ⓐ sapport
- Ⓑ saport
- Ⓒ support
- Ⓓ suport

Sample B:
- Ⓔ salid
- Ⓕ saled
- Ⓖ salud
- Ⓗ salad

1.
- Ⓐ ballut
- Ⓑ balet
- Ⓒ ballot
- Ⓓ ballat

2.
- Ⓔ canvis
- Ⓕ canvas
- Ⓖ canvus
- Ⓗ canves

3.
- Ⓐ morsle
- Ⓑ morsal
- Ⓒ morsil
- Ⓓ morsel

4.
- Ⓔ severe
- Ⓕ suvere
- Ⓖ savere
- Ⓗ sivere

5.
- Ⓐ standerd
- Ⓑ standord
- Ⓒ standard
- Ⓓ standurd

6.
- Ⓔ effert
- Ⓕ effurt
- Ⓖ effort
- Ⓗ effart

7.
- Ⓐ applause
- Ⓑ applawse
- Ⓒ aplause
- Ⓓ aplawse

8.
- Ⓔ albim
- Ⓕ album
- Ⓖ albom
- Ⓗ albam

9.
- Ⓐ nuisence
- Ⓑ nuisonce
- Ⓒ nuisance
- Ⓓ nuisince

10.
- Ⓔ opeal
- Ⓕ epeal
- Ⓖ uppeal
- Ⓗ appeal

11.
- Ⓐ judgment
- Ⓑ jugment
- Ⓒ judgmant
- Ⓓ jugmant

12.
- Ⓔ cenfess
- Ⓕ canfess
- Ⓖ cunfess
- Ⓗ confess

13.
- Ⓐ pondor
- Ⓑ ponder
- Ⓒ pondar
- Ⓓ pondir

14.
- Ⓔ pirhaps
- Ⓕ purhaps
- Ⓖ perhaps
- Ⓗ parhaps

15.
- Ⓐ sispend
- Ⓑ saspend
- Ⓒ sespend
- Ⓓ suspend

16.
- Ⓔ stubburn
- Ⓕ stubborn
- Ⓖ stubbarn
- Ⓗ stubbirn

17.
- Ⓐ ballad
- Ⓑ ballid
- Ⓒ ballud
- Ⓓ balled

18.
- Ⓔ sappose
- Ⓕ suppose
- Ⓖ seppose
- Ⓗ sippose

19.
- Ⓐ randum
- Ⓑ randim
- Ⓒ random
- Ⓓ randem

20.
- Ⓔ callide
- Ⓕ collide
- Ⓖ cellide
- Ⓗ cullide

Words with Silent Letters

Pretest Directions

Fold back the paper along the dotted line. Use the blanks to write each word as it is read aloud. When you finish the test, unfold the paper. Use the list at the right to correct any spelling mistakes. Practice the words you missed for the Posttest.

To Parents

Here are the results of your child's weekly spelling Pretest. You can help your child study for the Posttest by following these simple steps for each word on the word list:

1. Read the word to your child.

2. Have your child write the word, saying each letter as it is written.

3. Say each letter of the word as your child checks the spelling.

4. If a mistake has been made, have your child read each letter of the correctly spelled word aloud, and then repeat steps 1–3.

#		Word
1.	_____	1. headlights
2.	_____	2. rustle
3.	_____	3. calmly
4.	_____	4. yolk
5.	_____	5. nightmare
6.	_____	6. moisten
7.	_____	7. drought
8.	_____	8. resign
9.	_____	9. knack
10.	_____	10. condemn
11.	_____	11. bristle
12.	_____	12. doughnut
13.	_____	13. hasten
14.	_____	14. acknowledge
15.	_____	15. reign
16.	_____	16. salmon
17.	_____	17. nestle
18.	_____	18. align
19.	_____	19. almond
20.	_____	20. wrought

Challenge Words

_____ capsule

_____ interior

_____ lifeboats

_____ portholes

_____ severed

Name_____ Date_____

Words with Silent Letters

Using the Word Study Steps

1. LOOK at the word.
2. SAY the word aloud.
3. STUDY the letters in the word.
4. WRITE the word.
5. CHECK the word.

   Did you spell the word right?
   If not, go back to step 1.

Spelling Tip

Use a secret pronunciation of your own to help you spell some hard words.

moisten	/mō **is ten**/
yolk	/yōlk/
bristle	/bris **til**/
knack	/**kə** nak/

Scrambled Words

Unscramble the letters to make spelling words.

1. esrngi _____
2. mocdnne _____
3. lhtgsihdae _____
4. tsimone _____
5. trslue _____
6. grmathine _____
7. mallyc _____
8. loyk _____
9. gurothd _____
10. cankk _____
11. kdeelgwonca _____
12. hogwrut _____
13. giner _____
14. lonmad _____
15. nolmas _____
16. telsen _____
17. silrbet _____
18. gilan _____
19. thanes _____
20. htuodnug _____

To Parents or Helpers:

Using the Word Study Steps above as your child comes across any new words will help him or her learn to spell words effectively. Review the steps as you both go over this week's spelling words.

Go over the Spelling Tip with your child. Ask your child to say the secret pronunciations of the words in the Spelling Tip out loud. See if he or she can make up secret pronunciations for any of the spelling words.

Help your child complete the word scramble.

Words with Silent Letters

headlights	nightmare	knack	hasten	nestle
rustle	moisten	condemn	acknowledge	align
calmly	drought	bristle	reign	almond
yolk	resign	doughnut	salmon	wrought

Write the spelling words that contain these silent letters:

gh

1. _____

2. _____

3. _____

4. _____

5. _____

k

6. _____

7. _____

g

8. _____

9. _____

10. _____

l

11. _____

12. _____

13. _____

14. _____

t

15. _____

16. _____

17. _____

18. _____

19. _____

n

20. _____

Rhyming Words

A word that has silent letters can rhyme with words that are spelled very differently.
Write the spelling word that rhymes with the words below.

21. vessel _____

23. shout _____

22. joke _____

24. main _____

Words with Silent Letters

headlights	nightmare	knack	hasten	nestle
rustle	moisten	condemn	acknowledge	align
calmly	drought	bristle	reign	almond
yolk	resign	doughnut	salmon	wrought

Complete each sentence below with a spelling word.

1. Every _____ in my toothbrush is bent.

2. Make sure that he is guilty before you _____ him.

3. Pet the stray cat _____ or you will frighten him.

4. He has a real _____ for getting children to laugh.

5. I was disappointed when he did not _____ my help.

6. The kitten likes to _____ in my arms.

7. This table was _____ way back in the 1600s.

8. I was blinded by the bright _____ of the passing car.

Word Match

Write the spelling word that means the same as the word or phrase below.

9. dampen _____

10. quit _____

11. quicken _____

12. dry weather _____

13. fried cake _____

14. adjust _____

15. an oval nut _____

16. bad dream _____

17. kind of fish _____

18. egg center _____

19. ruling time _____

20. fluttering sound _____

118 **Challenge Extension:** Have students illustrate the meaning of each Challenge Word, exchange papers, and label each other's illustrations with the correct challenge words.

Grade 6/Unit 4
Exploring the Titanic 20

Words with Silent Letters

Proofreading Activity
There are six spelling mistakes in the paragraph below. Circle each misspelled word.
Write the words correctly on the lines below.

For some passengers, a cruise aboard Titanic had long been a dream.
In an instant, it turned into a nitmare. The iceberg took only seconds to smash into
the hull and condem many passengers to death. Unfortunately, the ship did not
have enough lifeboats. It took courage for the men to resine themselves to death.
They loaded the women and children into the boats. Then they camly waited for the
boat to sink. Many years later, Alvin's headlites showed explorers the destruction
the iceberg had rought.

1. _____ 3. _____ 5. _____

2. _____ 4. _____ 6. _____

Writing Activity
Write a journal entry a survivor of the Titanic might have written, describing the events
of the evening. Use at least four spelling words.

_____

_____

_____

_____

Words with Silent Letters

Look at the words in each set below. One word in each set is spelled correctly. Use a pencil to fill in the circle next to the correct word. Before you begin, look at the sample sets of words. Sample A has been done for you. Do Sample B by yourself. When you are sure you know what to do, you may go on with the rest of the page.

Sample A:
- Ⓐ fite
- Ⓑ figt
- Ⓒ fight
- Ⓓ fihte

Sample B:
- Ⓔ bought
- Ⓕ bot
- Ⓖ bougt
- Ⓗ bouht

1. Ⓐ yoek
Ⓑ yoak
Ⓒ yolk
Ⓓ yowk

6. Ⓔ reighn
Ⓕ rayn
Ⓖ reign
Ⓗ raign

11. Ⓐ rustle
Ⓑ rusle
Ⓒ russel
Ⓓ rustel

16. Ⓔ nitemare
Ⓕ nightmare
Ⓖ nigtmare
Ⓗ nihgtmare

2. Ⓔ resine
Ⓕ resign
Ⓖ resighn
Ⓗ ressin

7. Ⓐ headlights
Ⓑ hedlights
Ⓒ headligts
Ⓓ hedligts

12. Ⓔ almund
Ⓕ aumond
Ⓖ awmond
Ⓗ almond

17. Ⓐ bristle
Ⓑ brissle
Ⓒ brissel
Ⓓ bristel

3. Ⓐ drout
Ⓑ drowt
Ⓒ drougt
Ⓓ drought

8. Ⓔ aline
Ⓕ align
Ⓖ alighn
Ⓗ allin

13. Ⓐ sammon
Ⓑ salmon
Ⓒ sammen
Ⓓ salmen

18. Ⓔ nestel
Ⓕ nestle
Ⓖ nessle
Ⓗ nessel

4. Ⓔ knack
Ⓕ nack
Ⓖ knak
Ⓗ nak

9. Ⓐ moisin
Ⓑ moisen
Ⓒ moisten
Ⓓ moistin

14. Ⓔ condem
Ⓕ condemm
Ⓖ condemn
Ⓗ cundemn

19. Ⓐ rought
Ⓑ raught
Ⓒ wrought
Ⓓ wraught

5. Ⓐ caumly
Ⓑ camnly
Ⓒ calmly
Ⓓ comly

10. Ⓔ dounut
Ⓕ downut
Ⓖ doughnut
Ⓗ dowghnut

15. Ⓐ acknowlege
Ⓑ acnowledge
Ⓒ aknowledge
Ⓓ acknowledge

20. Ⓔ hastin
Ⓕ hasten
Ⓖ hasen
Ⓗ hascen

Words from Science

Pretest Directions

Fold back the paper along the dotted line. Use the blanks to write each word as it is read aloud. When you finish the test, unfold the paper. Use the list at the right to correct any spelling mistakes. Practice the words you missed for the Posttest.

To Parents

Here are the results of your child's weekly spelling Pretest. You can help your child study for the Posttest by following these simple steps for each word on the word list:

1. Read the word to your child.

2. Have your child write the word, saying each letter as it is written.

3. Say each letter of the word as your child checks the spelling.

4. If a mistake has been made, have your child read each letter of the correctly spelled word aloud, and then repeat steps 1–3.

1. _____	1. rocket
2. _____	2. crater
3. _____	3. telescopes
4. _____	4. hurtle
5. _____	5. revolve
6. _____	6. orbiting
7. _____	7. comet
8. _____	8. meteors
9. _____	9. astronomers
10. _____	10. rotate
11. _____	11. altitude
12. _____	12. constellation
13. _____	13. galaxy
14. _____	14. odyssey
15. _____	15. alien
16. _____	16. eclipse
17. _____	17. thermal
18. _____	18. asteroid
19. _____	19. planetarium
20. _____	20. variable

Challenge Words

_____	hydrogen
_____	lunar
_____	magnetic
_____	quantities
_____	sensor

Words from Science

Using the Word Study Steps

1. LOOK at the word.
2. SAY the word aloud.
3. STUDY the letters in the word.
4. WRITE the word.
5. CHECK the word.

   Did you spell the word right?
   If not, go back to step 1.

Spelling Tip

It may be helpful to first divide the word into syllables and then spell each syllable.

con stel la tion

as tron o mers

plan e tar i um

Find the Words

Draw a line around each spelling word.

```
d c o m e t k m e t e o r s s o r b i t i n g p

a l t i t u d e w t a s t r o n o m e r s h p k

g r e v o l v e m c r a t e r n m g a l a x y h

w q r t e l e s c o p e s m a h u r t l e f c v

e r o c k e t f p c o n s t e l l a t i o n l p

v a r i a b l e m n o p l a n e t a r i u m f g

r a l i e n r l o d y s s e y p u t h e r m a l

e c l i p s e r a s t e r o i d u r o t a t e a
```

To Parents or Helpers:

Using the Word Study Steps above as your child comes across any new words will help him or her learn to spell words effectively. Review the steps as you both go over this week's spelling words.

Go over the Spelling Tip with your child. Ask your child to divide other spelling words into syllables and then spell each syllable.

Help your child identify the spelling words in each row.

Words from Science

rocket	revolve	astronomers	galaxy	thermal
crater	orbiting	rotate	odyssey	asteroid
telescopes	comet	altitude	alien	planetarium
hurtle	meteors	constellation	eclipse	variable

Using your dictionary, find the syllable with the primary stress in each spelling word.
Then write the spelling word under the vowel sound to which its primary stress
syllable belongs.

Short Vowel   **Long Vowel**

1. _____   11. _____

2. _____   12. _____

3. _____   13. _____

4. _____   14. _____

5. _____   15. _____

6. _____   **R-Controlled Vowel**

7. _____   16. _____

8. _____   17. _____

9. _____   18. _____

10. _____   19. _____

20. _____

Rhyming Words
Write the spelling word that rhymes with the words below.

21. skater _____   23. pocket _____

22. dissolve _____   24. fertile _____

Words from Science

rocket	revolve	astronomers	galaxy	thermal
crater	orbiting	rotate	odyssey	asteroid
telescopes	comet	altitude	alien	planetarium
hurtle	meteors	constellation	eclipse	variable

Complete each sentence below with a spelling word.

1. Falling quickly to Earth, the _____ burned before landing.

2. The _____ looked like a star with a tail traveling across the sky.

3. Mark went to the _____ to learn about planets.

4. They looked through _____ to see the moon.

5. They listened while _____ told about the stars.

6. Maria picked out stars in her favorite _____.

7. The _____ in which we live is called the Milky Way.

8. An _____ planet always follows the exact same path.

9. An _____ is a planet that is very small.

10. Earth takes 365 days to _____ around the sun.

11. Earth takes 24 hours to _____ once on its axis.

Write the spelling word that means the same as the word or phrase below.

12. missile _____

13. journey _____

14. overshadow _____

15. hollow area _____

16. from outer space _____

17. move rapidly _____

18. cause heat _____

19. changeable _____

20. height _____

Challenge Extension: Have students use a dictionary to define each Challenge Word and write one sentence for each.

124

Grade 6/Unit 4
Back to the Moon

20

Words from Science

Proofreading Activity

There are six spelling mistakes in the paragraph below. Circle each misspelled word.
Write the words correctly on the lines below.

People have long dreamed of visiting another galixy. However, scientists have

not developed a rockit that can take humans out of the solar system. Even a trip to

the moon is a major odysey. Astronmers can still learn much about distant stars.

The public can see them through telscopes in a planeterium.

1. _____   3. _____   5. _____

2. _____   4. _____   6. _____

Writing Activity

Write about planning for a trip to the moon. Use at least four spelling words.

_____

_____

_____

_____

Words from Science

Look at the words in each set below. One word in each set is spelled correctly. Use a pencil to fill in the circle next to the correct word. Before you begin, look at the sample sets of words. Sample A has been done for you. Do Sample B by yourself. When you are sure you know what to do, you may go on with the rest of the page.

Sample A:
- Ⓐ history
- Ⓑ hisory
- Ⓒ histry
- Ⓓ histery

Sample B:
- Ⓔ favvor
- Ⓕ faver
- Ⓖ favor
- Ⓗ faivor

1.
- Ⓐ roatate
- Ⓑ rottate
- Ⓒ rotate
- Ⓓ rowtate

2.
- Ⓔ hertle
- Ⓕ hurtle
- Ⓖ hirtle
- Ⓗ hurtel

3.
- Ⓐ ailen
- Ⓑ alian
- Ⓒ allien
- Ⓓ alien

4.
- Ⓔ constellation
- Ⓕ constelation
- Ⓖ constallation
- Ⓗ constalation

5.
- Ⓐ commet
- Ⓑ comitt
- Ⓒ comet
- Ⓓ comit

6.
- Ⓔ astroid
- Ⓕ asturoid
- Ⓖ asteroid
- Ⓗ astiroid

7.
- Ⓐ rocket
- Ⓑ roccet
- Ⓒ raucket
- Ⓓ rauket

8.
- Ⓔ telscopes
- Ⓕ telescopes
- Ⓖ teliscopes
- Ⓗ telascopes

9.
- Ⓐ planaterium
- Ⓑ planetrium
- Ⓒ planetarium
- Ⓓ planatarium

10.
- Ⓔ orbitting
- Ⓕ orbetting
- Ⓖ orbeting
- Ⓗ orbiting

11.
- Ⓐ meteors
- Ⓑ metears
- Ⓒ metiors
- Ⓓ meeteors

12.
- Ⓔ varyable
- Ⓕ varyible
- Ⓖ varriable
- Ⓗ variable

13.
- Ⓐ astronmers
- Ⓑ astronomers
- Ⓒ astronamers
- Ⓓ astronemers

14.
- Ⓔ odissey
- Ⓕ odissy
- Ⓖ odyssey
- Ⓗ odysey

15.
- Ⓐ alditude
- Ⓑ aldatude
- Ⓒ altatude
- Ⓓ altitude

16.
- Ⓔ eclipss
- Ⓕ eclipse
- Ⓖ eclipce
- Ⓗ eclypse

17.
- Ⓐ crater
- Ⓑ crator
- Ⓒ craiter
- Ⓓ craitor

18.
- Ⓔ galixy
- Ⓕ galaxy
- Ⓖ gallaxy
- Ⓗ galexy

19.
- Ⓐ revalve
- Ⓑ revulve
- Ⓒ revolve
- Ⓓ rivolve

20.
- Ⓔ thermel
- Ⓕ thermal
- Ⓖ thermle
- Ⓗ thurmal

Grade 6/Unit 4 Review Test

Read each sentence. If an underlined word is spelled wrong, fill in the circle that goes with that word. If no word is spelled wrong, fill in the circle below NONE.

Read Sample A and do Sample B.

A. <u>Plants</u> are affected by the sun in the <u>solar</u> <u>system</u>.
    A   B   C

                                             NONE
A. Ⓐ   Ⓑ   Ⓒ   ⬤

B. <u>Astronomers</u> can <u>obsurve</u> the path of a <u>comet</u>.
       E   F   G

                                             NONE
B. Ⓔ   Ⓕ   Ⓖ   Ⓗ

1. Add the egg <u>yoak</u> to the <u>chestnut</u> <u>doughnut</u> batter.
               A   B   C

                                             NONE
1. Ⓐ   Ⓑ   Ⓒ   Ⓓ

2. The <u>superior</u> egg <u>yolk</u> improved his <u>chestnut</u> cake.
        E   F   G

                                             NONE
2. Ⓔ   Ⓕ   Ⓖ   Ⓗ

3. His <u>superior</u> <u>nack</u> for baking helped him <u>reign</u> as king of bakers.
        A   B   C

                                             NONE
3. Ⓐ   Ⓑ   Ⓒ   Ⓓ

4. The <u>ballad</u> was about a <u>chesnut</u> and a <u>doughnut</u>.
        E   F   G

                                             NONE
4. Ⓔ   Ⓕ   Ⓖ   Ⓗ

5. We will <u>suspend</u> conversation and <u>ponder</u> the issues in <u>unisen</u>.
            A   B   C

                                             NONE
5. Ⓐ   Ⓑ   Ⓒ   Ⓓ

6. We spend our <u>leisure</u> time in an <u>erban</u> <u>doughnut</u> café.
                E   F   G

                                             NONE
6. Ⓔ   Ⓕ   Ⓖ   Ⓗ

7. During his <u>reign</u>, the <u>shrunkin</u> staff had <u>leisure</u> time.
              A   B   C

                                             NONE
7. Ⓐ   Ⓑ   Ⓒ   Ⓓ

8. People <u>condemn</u> him for his <u>supersticious</u> <u>manner</u>.
              E   F   G

                                           NONE
8. Ⓔ   Ⓕ   Ⓖ   Ⓗ

9. <u>Urban</u> people <u>condemn</u> skateboards as a <u>nuisance</u>.
      A   B   C

                                           NONE
9. Ⓐ   Ⓑ   Ⓒ   Ⓓ

10. It is a <u>nuisince</u> to <u>collide</u> with a <u>leisure</u> chair.
         E   F   G

                                           NONE
10. Ⓔ   Ⓕ   Ⓖ   Ⓗ

Go on ➡

Grade 6/Unit 4 Review Test

11. At a <u>planatarium</u> I saw a <u>constellation</u> in the <u>galaxy</u>.
      A   B   C
11. Ⓐ Ⓑ Ⓒ Ⓓ NONE

12. The <u>galaxy</u> appears to <u>revolve</u> at the <u>planeterium</u>.
     E   F   G
12. Ⓔ Ⓕ Ⓖ Ⓗ NONE

13. At the <u>planetarium</u> I saw planets in the <u>galaxy</u> <u>revovle</u>.
         A   B   C
13. Ⓐ Ⓑ Ⓒ Ⓓ NONE

14. The <u>shrunken</u> <u>jumbles</u> of light became a <u>constellation</u>.
        E   F   G
14. Ⓔ Ⓕ Ⓖ Ⓗ NONE

15. Are <u>meteors</u>, in a <u>manner</u>, part of a <u>constelation</u>?
        A   B   C
15. Ⓐ Ⓑ Ⓒ Ⓓ NONE

16. <u>Metoers</u> can <u>collide</u> with Earth in an <u>urban</u> area.
      E   F   G
16. Ⓔ Ⓕ Ⓖ Ⓗ NONE

17. Cindy is <u>superstitious</u> about how <u>meteors</u> <u>collide</u>.
           A   B   C
17. Ⓐ Ⓑ Ⓒ Ⓓ NONE

18. A king can <u>ponder</u> how Earth will <u>revolve</u> during his <u>rane</u>.
           E   F   G
18. Ⓔ Ⓕ Ⓖ Ⓗ NONE

19. The <u>superstitious</u> choir sang a <u>balad</u> in <u>unison</u>.
        A   B   C
19. Ⓐ Ⓑ Ⓒ Ⓓ NONE

20. <u>Suspend</u> all activities and <u>condem</u> them as a <u>nuisance</u>.
    E   F   G
20. Ⓔ Ⓕ Ⓖ Ⓗ NONE

21. The <u>glacier</u> has <u>shrunken</u> into <u>jumbels</u> of ice.
      A   B   C
21. Ⓐ Ⓑ Ⓒ Ⓓ NONE

22. They had a <u>knack</u> for singing that <u>ballad</u> in <u>unison</u>.
           E   F   G
22. Ⓔ Ⓕ Ⓖ Ⓗ NONE

23. She <u>jumbles</u> that egg <u>yolk</u> in a serious <u>maner</u>.
        A   B   C
23. Ⓐ Ⓑ Ⓒ Ⓓ NONE

24. She has a <u>superier</u> <u>knack</u> for sailing by a <u>glacier</u>.
           E   F   G
24. Ⓔ Ⓕ Ⓖ Ⓗ NONE

25. Why <u>suspend</u> sailing to <u>pondor</u> the <u>glacier</u>?
        A   B   C
25. Ⓐ Ⓑ Ⓒ Ⓓ NONE

Compound Words

Pretest Directions

Fold back the paper along the dotted line. Use the blanks to write each word as it is read aloud. When you finish the test, unfold the paper. Use the list at the right to correct any spelling mistakes. Practice the words you missed for the Posttest.

To Parents

Here are the results of your child's weekly spelling Pretest. You can help your child study for the Posttest by following these simple steps for each word on the word list:

1. Read the word to your child.

2. Have your child write the word, saying each letter as it is written.

3. Say each letter of the word as your child checks the spelling.

4. If a mistake has been made, have your child read each letter of the correctly spelled word aloud, and then repeat steps 1–3.

1. _____	1. newborn
2. _____	2. twenty-one
3. _____	3. common sense
4. _____	4. old-fashioned
5. _____	5. question mark
6. _____	6. teacup
7. _____	7. tablecloth
8. _____	8. ready-made
9. _____	9. bathrobe
10. _____	10. science fiction
11. _____	11. apartment houses
12. _____	12. brother-in-law
13. _____	13. fire escape
14. _____	14. applesauce
15. _____	15. self-reliant
16. _____	16. index finger
17. _____	17. cross-country
18. _____	18. foolproof
19. _____	19. contact lens
20. _____	20. silkworms

Challenge Words

_____ banister

_____ grudged

_____ porcelain

_____ rhythmically

_____ truce

Compound Words

Using the Word Study Steps

1. LOOK at the word.
2. SAY the word aloud.
3. STUDY the letters in the word.
4. WRITE the word.
5. CHECK the word.

   Did you spell the word right?
   If not, go back to step 1.

Spelling Tip

When you write out numbers between 21 and 99, remember to include the hyphen.

twenty-one   thirty-six

eighty-seven

Finish the Word

Complete each word below to form a spelling word.

1. new_____

2. _____-one

3. common _____

4. old-_____

5. _____ mark

6. tea_____

7. _____cloth

8. ready-_____

9. _____robe

10. science _____

11. _____ houses

12. _____-in-law

13. fire _____

14. apple_____

15. _____-reliant

16. index _____

17. _____-country

18. fool_____

19. _____ lens

20. silk_____

To Parents or Helpers:

   Using the Word Study Steps above as your child comes across any new words will help him or her spell words effectively. Review the steps as you both go over this week's spelling words.

   Go over the Spelling Tip with your child. Take turns writing out numbers, inserting the hyphen.

   Help your child complete the spelling exercise by completing each spelling word.

Compound Words

newborn	question mark	bathrobe	fire escape	cross-country
twenty-one	teacup	science fiction	applesauce	foolproof
common sense	tablecloth	apartment houses	self-reliant	contact lens
old-fashioned	ready-made	brother-in-law	index finger	silkworms

Sort each spelling word according to whether it is written as one word, as two words, or with a hyphen. Write each word on the appropriate line below.

One Word:

1. _____
2. _____
3. _____
4. _____
5. _____
6. _____
7. _____

Two Words:

8. _____
9. _____
10. _____
11. _____
12. _____
13. _____
14. _____

Hyphenated:

15. _____
16. _____
17. _____

18. _____
19. _____
20. _____

Compound Words

newborn	question mark	bathrobe	fire escape	cross-country
twenty-one	teacup	science fiction	applesauce	foolproof
common sense	tablecloth	apartment houses	self-reliant	contact lens
old-fashioned	ready-made	brother-in-law	index finger	silkworms

Write the spelling word that best completes each sentence.

1. I can't find my left _____ so I'll wear my glasses.

2. Those _____ are caterpillars.

3. I put some milk in a _____ and fed it to the kitten.

4. People in cities live in big _____.

5. Most people point with the _____.

6. I use the _____ as a balcony on hot days.

7. You should end your questions with a _____.

8. My mom served _____ with the pork chops.

Synonyms and Antonyms
Write the spelling word which is a synonym (S) or antonym (A) of each word or words below.

9. modern (A) _____

10. made to order (A) _____

11. infant (S) _____

12. practical judgment (S) _____

13. dependent (A) _____

14. simple (S) _____

Finish the Set
Write the spelling word which belongs with each group of words below.

15. nineteen, twenty, _____

16. napkin, napkin holder, _____

17. fantasy, mystery, _____

18. cousin, sister, _____

19. swimming, soccer, _____

20. pajamas, nightgown, _____

Challenge Extension: Have students take turns using each challenge word in a sentence.

Grade 6/Unit 5
Child of the Owl
20

Compound Words

Proofreading Activity

There are six spelling mistakes in this paragraph. Circle the misspelled words. Write
the words correctly on the lines below.

    As Phil drove the car, I looked at all the tall apartment-houses in the

neighborhood. We parked at one group of buildings. Phil pointed with his

indexfinger toward the top floor. "That's where Paw Paw lives," he said. I had heard

that Paw Paw was old-fasioned and extremely selfreliant. She answered the door in

an old bath-robe and black slippers. I felt a bit nervous at first, but as we started

talking I felt more comfortable. It was commonsense. She was my grandmother

after all!

1. _____   3. _____   5. _____

2. _____   4. _____   6. _____

Writing Activity

If you had to move, which older friend or relative would you most like to move in with?
Why? Write a letter to that person, telling him or her why you would like to move in.
Use four spelling words.

_____

_____

_____

_____

Compound Words

Look at the words in each set below. One word in each set is spelled correctly. Use a pencil to fill in the circle next to the correct word. Before you begin, look at the sample sets of words. Sample A has been done for you. Do Sample B by yourself. When you are sure you know what to do, you may go on with the rest of the page.

Sample A:
- Ⓐ honey-bee
- Ⓑ hunny bee
- Ⓒ honey bee
- ⬤ honeybee

Sample B:
- Ⓔ ice-cream
- Ⓕ ice cream
- Ⓖ icecream
- Ⓗ ise cream

1. Ⓐ contact lens / Ⓑ contackt lens / Ⓒ contact lenz / Ⓓ contackt lenz

2. Ⓔ brotherinlaw / Ⓕ brother inlaw / Ⓖ brother in law / Ⓗ brother-in-law

3. Ⓐ newborne / Ⓑ new borne / Ⓒ newborn / Ⓓ new born

4. Ⓔ tea cup / Ⓕ teacup / Ⓖ tee cup / Ⓗ teecup

5. Ⓐ apartmint houses / Ⓑ apartmunt houses / Ⓒ apartment houses / Ⓓ appartment houses

6. Ⓔ twentywon / Ⓕ twenty one / Ⓖ twenty-one / Ⓗ twenty-won

7. Ⓐ silk worms / Ⓑ silkworms / Ⓒ silk wurms / Ⓓ silkwurms

8. Ⓔ foolproof / Ⓕ fool-proof / Ⓖ fool proof / Ⓗ foolproofe

9. Ⓐ batherobe / Ⓑ bathe-robe / Ⓒ bathrobe / Ⓓ bath-robe

10. Ⓔ common-sense / Ⓕ commin-sense / Ⓖ common sense / Ⓗ commin sense

11. Ⓐ old fashioned / Ⓑ oldfashunned / Ⓒ old-fashunned / Ⓓ old-fashioned

12. Ⓔ questionmark / Ⓕ question-mark / Ⓖ questione-mark / Ⓗ question mark

13. Ⓐ readymake / Ⓑ ready-made / Ⓒ reddy-made / Ⓓ readdy made

14. Ⓔ apple sauce / Ⓕ appllesauce / Ⓖ applesauce / Ⓗ aplesauce

15. Ⓐ table clothe / Ⓑ table cloth / Ⓒ tableclothe / Ⓓ tablecloth

16. Ⓔ sience-fiction / Ⓕ science-fiction / Ⓖ sience fiction / Ⓗ science fiction

17. Ⓐ cross-country / Ⓑ cross country / Ⓒ chross-country / Ⓓ chross country

18. Ⓔ selfreliant / Ⓕ sellf-reliant / Ⓖ selff reliant / Ⓗ self-reliant

19. Ⓐ firescape / Ⓑ fir escape / Ⓒ fire escape / Ⓓ fire escap

20. Ⓔ index fingir / Ⓕ index-fingir / Ⓖ index finger / Ⓗ index-finger

Homophones and Homographs

Pretest Directions

Fold back the paper along the dotted line. Use the blanks to write each word as it is read aloud. When you finish the test, unfold the paper. Use the list at the right to correct any spelling mistakes. Practice the words you missed for the Posttest.

To Parents

Here are the results of your child's weekly spelling Pretest. You can help your child study for the Posttest by following these simple steps for each word on the word list:

1. Read the word to your child.

2. Have your child write the word, saying each letter as it is written.

3. Say each letter of the word as your child checks the spelling.

4. If a mistake has been made, have your child read each letter of the correctly spelled word aloud, and then repeat steps 1–3.

1. _____	1. straight
2. _____	2. dove
3. _____	3. shear
4. _____	4. hire
5. _____	5. swallow
6. _____	6. racket
7. _____	7. strait
8. _____	8. sheer
9. _____	9. hamper
10. _____	10. higher
11. _____	11. vain
12. _____	12. cereal
13. _____	13. principal
14. _____	14. refrain
15. _____	15. kernel
16. _____	16. bass
17. _____	17. vein
18. _____	18. principle
19. _____	19. colonel
20. _____	20. serial

Challenge Words

_____ ferocious

_____ lavishly

_____ reassure

_____ thunderous

_____ waving

Name_____ Date_____

Homophones and Homographs

Using the Word Study Steps

1. LOOK at the word.
2. SAY the word aloud.
3. STUDY the letters in the word.
4. WRITE the word.
5. CHECK the word.

   Did you spell the word right?
   If not, go back to step 1.

Spelling Tip

Learn the meanings of common homophones to help you use the right one in your writing.

I scored **higher** than you on the math test.

The restaurant will **hire** two new waiters.

Word Scramble

Unscramble each set of letters to make a spelling word.

1. ttasri _____
2. rearfin _____
3. ihhger _____
4. sbsa _____
5. lloocen _____
6. evod _____
7. awollws _____
8. hares _____
9. nvie _____
10. repham _____

11. lecera _____
12. ireh _____
13. lappiinrc _____
14. lekren _____
15. triastgh _____
16. siearl _____
17. ershe _____
18. tekrac _____
19. cipprilen _____
20. ainv _____

To Parents or Helpers:

   Using the Word Study Steps above as your child comes across any new words will help him or her spell well. Review the steps as you both go over this week's spelling words.

   Go over the Spelling Tip with your child. Write other sentences using homophones.

   Help your child unscramble the spelling words.

EXPLORE THE PATTERN

Homophones and Homographs

straight	swallow	hamper	principal	vein
dove	racket	higher	refrain	principle
shear	strait	vain	kernel	colonel
hire	sheer	cereal	bass	serial

Sort the spelling words into homophone pairs and homographs. Write the words on the appropriate lines below.

Homophones

1. _____   9. _____

2. _____   10. _____

3. _____   11. _____

4. _____   12. _____

5. _____   13. _____

6. _____   14. _____

7. _____

8. _____

Homographs

15. _____   18. _____

16. _____   19. _____

17. _____   20. _____

Name_____ Date_____

Homophones and Homographs

straight	swallow	hamper	principal	vein
dove	racket	higher	refrain	principle
shear	strait	vain	kernel	colonel
hire	sheer	cereal	bass	serial

Meaning Match-Up
Write the spelling word which matches each definition below.

1. not curly _____

2. to clip or cut _____

3. to employ _____

4 conceited _____

5. thin waterway _____

6. blood vessel _____

7. grain breakfast food _____

8. chief _____

9. military officer _____

10. very thin _____

11 law or belief _____

12. seed of plants _____

13. further upward _____

14. story part _____

More Than One Meaning
Read the definitions below. Then write the letters of the two definitions which correspond with each homograph below.

a. to engulf

b. opposite of treble

c. perching bird

d. to hold oneself back

e. plunged headfirst

f. to impede

g. pigeon

h. a large basket

i. type of fish

j. paddle

k. recurring verse

l. clamor

1. dove _____ _____

2. racket _____ _____

3. refrain _____ _____

4. swallow _____ _____

5. bass _____ _____

6. hamper _____ _____

Challenge Extension: Have students write a short fairy tale using each Challenge Word.

Grade 6/Unit 5
Bellerophon and the Flying Horse 20

Homophones and Homographs

Proofreading Activity
There are six spelling mistakes in this paragraph. Circle the misspelled words. Write the words correctly on the lines below.

The King of Lycia told Bellerophon he wanted to hiar him for a mission—to slay the Chimera. However, the king did not tell Bellerophon that his journey would be in vein. All the men that had tried to kill the Chimera had died in the attempt. Bellerophon set strait off without fear. He flew on Pegasus, the winged horse, for miles until he heard a rackit in a nearby valley. Bellerophon saw that the Chimera had three horrible heads, which tried to swalow him whole! Bellerophon rode Pegasus hire into the sky and then they dove towards the monster, killing one head with each blow.

1. _____   3. _____   5. _____

2. _____   4. _____   6. _____

Writing Activity
What is your favorite fairy tale or myth about an evil king or a brave hero or heroine? Rewrite it, using at least four spelling words.

_____

_____

_____

_____

Homophones and Homographs

Look at the words in each set below. One word in each set is spelled correctly. Use a pencil to fill in the circle next to the correct word. Before you begin, look at the sample sets of words. Sample A has been done for you. Do Sample B by yourself. When you are sure you know what to do, you may go on with the rest of the page.

Sample A:
- (A) lier
- (B) lyer
- (C) liar
- (D) liur

Sample B:
- (E) bridel
- (F) bridall
- (G) bridell
- (H) bridal

1. (A) dove
   (B) duv
   (C) dovv
   (D) duvv

2. (E) vain
   (F) vaine
   (G) vaen
   (H) vayn

3. (A) prinsipul
   (B) principul
   (C) principal
   (D) principull

4. (E) bass
   (F) bahss
   (G) bas
   (H) basce

5. (A) rackit
   (B) raquit
   (C) racquit
   (D) racket

6. (E) hampur
   (F) hamper
   (G) hampir
   (H) hampurr

7. (A) hiar
   (B) hyre
   (C) hyer
   (D) hire

8. (E) kernel
   (F) kurnel
   (G) kurnil
   (H) kernil

9. (A) principell
   (B) prinsiple
   (C) principle
   (D) prinsaple

10. (E) strate
    (F) straite
    (G) straight
    (H) straighte

11. (A) cereall
    (B) cereal
    (C) cereeal
    (D) ceereal

12. (E) colonel
    (F) cornel
    (G) culonel
    (H) calonel

13. (A) sheere
    (B) scheer
    (C) scheere
    (D) sheer

14. (E) swalow
    (F) swallow
    (G) swalo
    (H) swallo

15. (A) reefrain
    (B) reefraine
    (C) refrain
    (D) refraine

16. (E) strate
    (F) strait
    (G) straite
    (H) strat

17. (A) hygher
    (B) hier
    (C) higher
    (D) highir

18. (E) vein
    (F) vayn
    (G) veine
    (H) veun

19. (A) shier
    (B) shere
    (C) sheerr
    (D) shear

20. (E) sereal
    (F) sureal
    (G) serial
    (H) seriale

Words with Suffixes

Pretest Directions

Fold back the paper along the dotted line. Use the blanks to write each word as it is read aloud. When you finish the test, unfold the paper. Use the list at the right to correct any spelling mistakes. Practice the words you missed for the Posttest.

To Parents

Here are the results of your child's weekly spelling Pretest. You can help your child study for the Posttest by following these simple steps for each word on the word list:

1. Read the word to your child.

2. Have your child write the word, saying each letter as it is written.

3. Say each letter of the word as your child checks the spelling.

4. If a mistake has been made, have your child read each letter of the correctly spelled word aloud, and then repeat steps 1–3.

#		Word
1.	____	1. electricity
2.	____	2. operation
3.	____	3. exploration
4.	____	4. flexible
5.	____	5. considerable
6.	____	6. combination
7.	____	7. gravity
8.	____	8. lovable
9.	____	9. permissible
10.	____	10. interruption
11.	____	11. reality
12.	____	12. conservation
13.	____	13. collectible
14.	____	14. abbreviation
15.	____	15. perspiration
16.	____	16. admirable
17.	____	17. anticipation
18.	____	18. festivity
19.	____	19. imaginable
20.	____	20. convertible

Challenge Words

____ bloodstream

____ compartment

____ deliberately

____ handshake

____ maneuvering

Words with Suffixes

Using the Word Study Steps

1. LOOK at the word.
2. SAY the word aloud.
3. STUDY the letters in the word.
4. WRITE the word.
5. CHECK the word.

   Did you spell the word right?
   If not, go back to step 1.

Spelling Tip

Remember to drop the final **e** before adding the suffix.

imagine = imaginable
admire = admirable
combine = combination

Related Word

Write the spelling word related to each word below.

1. electric _____
2. operate _____
3. explore _____
4. flex _____
5. consider _____
6. grave _____
7. love _____
8. permit _____
9. interrupt _____
10. real _____

11. conserve _____
12. collect _____
13. abbreviate _____
14. perspire _____
15. admire _____
16. anticipate _____
17. festive _____
18. imagine _____
19. convert _____
20. combine _____

To Parents or Helpers:
   Using the Word Study Steps above as your child comes across any new words will help him or her spell well. Review the steps as you both go over this week's spelling words.

   Go over the Spelling Tip with your child. Help your child identify other words that drop the final *e* before adding a suffix. Help your child find the spelling words in the puzzle.

Words with Suffixes

electricity	considerable	permissible	collectible	anticipation
operation	combination	interruption	abbreviation	festivity
exploration	gravity	reality	perspiration	imaginable
flexible	lovable	conservation	admirable	convertible

Write the spelling words with the following suffixes:

-ion

1. _____
2. _____
3. _____
4. _____

-ation

5. _____
6. _____
7. _____
8. _____

-ity

9. _____
10. _____
11. _____
12. _____

-able

13. _____
14. _____
15. _____
16. _____

-ible

17. _____
18. _____
19. _____
20. _____

Words with Suffixes

electricity	considerable	permissible	collectible	anticipation
operation	combination	interruption	abbreviation	festivity
exploration	gravity	reality	perspiration	imaginable
flexible	lovable	conservation	admirable	convertible

Word Meaning

Write the spelling word that matches each root word.

1. electric _____

2. operate _____

3. explore _____

4. flex _____

5. consider _____

6. real _____

7. grave _____

8. love _____

9. permit _____

10. interrupt _____

Sentence Completions

Write the spelling word which best completes each sentence.

1. Old coins and postage stamps are _____ items.

2. *Mr.* is an _____ of the word *Mister.*

3. We waited with _____ for the arrival of our guests.

4. They will have singers and musicians as part of the _____.

5. I have tried every _____ way to solve this puzzle.

6. This _____ sofa can also be used as a bed.

Synonyms

Write the spelling word with the same, or similar, meaning as each word below.

1. mixture _____

2. preservation _____

3. sweat _____

4. excellent _____

Challenge Extension: Challenge each student
to write a one-paragraph story using at least four of
144 the Challenge Words.

Grade 6/Unit 5
Adventure in Space 20

Words with Suffixes

Proofreading Activity

There are six spelling mistakes in this letter. Circle the misspelled words. Write the words correctly on the lines below.

Dear Tom,

As you know, I have been working in the field of space expliration without interuption for the past ten years. There have been considereable advances since then. Thanks to a better understanding of graveity, our current opiration is running smoothly. With a combination of hard work and admireable forethought, our space program has become a leader.

Thanks for all your encouragement!

Kathy

1. _____   3. _____   5. _____

2. _____   4. _____   6. _____

Writing Activity

Write a journal entry describing you taking a make-believe voyage into space. Use four spelling words.

_____

_____

_____

_____

Words with Suffixes

Look at the words in each set below. One word in each set is spelled correctly. Use a pencil to fill in the circle next to the correct word. Before you begin, look at the sample sets of words. Sample A has been done for you. Do Sample B by yourself. When you are sure you know what to do, you may go on with the rest of the page.

Sample A:
- (A) educasion
- (B) educcation
- (C) **education**
- (D) edducation

Sample B:
- (E) iritable
- (F) irretable
- (G) irritabel
- (H) irritable

1.
- (A) convertable
- (B) convertible
- (C) convirtable
- (D) convirtible

2.
- (E) abreeviation
- (F) abbreviation
- (G) abreeviashun
- (H) abbreviashun

3.
- (A) considderable
- (B) considderible
- (C) considerable
- (D) considerible

4.
- (E) interuption
- (F) intaruption
- (G) interruption
- (H) intarruption

5.
- (A) eelectricity
- (B) electrisity
- (C) eelectrisity
- (D) electricity

6.
- (E) conservation
- (F) consirvation
- (G) conservashun
- (H) consirvashun

7.
- (A) festivvitie
- (B) festivvity
- (C) festivitie
- (D) festivity

8.
- (E) loveble
- (F) lovable
- (G) loveible
- (H) lovible

9.
- (A) explaration
- (B) exploration
- (C) explarasion
- (D) explorasion

10.
- (E) admirable
- (F) admarable
- (G) admirrable
- (H) admarrable

11.
- (A) gravity
- (B) gravitee
- (C) gravitty
- (D) gravittee

12.
- (E) permissible
- (F) permissable
- (G) permisible
- (H) permisable

13.
- (A) anticipasion
- (B) anticipation
- (C) antisipation
- (D) antisipasion

14.
- (E) flexable
- (F) flexabble
- (G) flexibble
- (H) flexible

15.
- (A) combanation
- (B) combination
- (C) combanasion
- (D) combinnation

16.
- (E) imaginable
- (F) imajinable
- (G) imadginable
- (H) imaginible

17.
- (A) realitee
- (B) reallity
- (C) reality
- (D) reallitee

18.
- (E) perspirration
- (F) pirspirration
- (G) pirspiration
- (H) perspiration

19.
- (A) collectuble
- (B) collectible
- (C) colectable
- (D) colectible

20.
- (E) operration
- (F) opiration
- (G) operation
- (H) opperation

Words with Suffixes

Pretest Directions

Fold back the paper along the dotted line. Use the blanks to write each word as it is read aloud. When you finish the test, unfold the paper. Use the list at the right to correct any spelling mistakes. Practice the words you missed for the Posttest.

To Parents

Here are the results of your child's weekly spelling Pretest. You can help your child study for the Posttest by following these simple steps for each word on the word list:

1. Read the word to your child.
2. Have your child write the word, saying each letter as it is written.
3. Say each letter of the word as your child checks the spelling.
4. If a mistake has been made, have your child read each letter of the correctly spelled word aloud, and then repeat steps 1–3.

1. _____ 1. excellent
2. _____ 2. attendant
3. _____ 3. restless
4. _____ 4. disturbance
5. _____ 5. conference
6. _____ 6. moisten
7. _____ 7. annoyance
8. _____ 8. occupant
9. _____ 9. cleverness
10. _____ 10. reference
11. _____ 11. acquaintance
12. _____ 12. persistent
13. _____ 13. sightless
14. _____ 14. descendant
15. _____ 15. dizziness
16. _____ 16. occurrence
17. _____ 17. boundless
18. _____ 18. emptiness
19. _____ 19. correspondent
20. _____ 20. regardless

Challenge Words

_____ barley
_____ coincidences
_____ mufflers
_____ sheepishly
_____ sweeten

Words with Suffixes

Using the Word Study Steps

1. LOOK at the word
2. SAY the word aloud.
3. STUDY the letters in the word.
4. WRITE the word.
5. CHECK the word.

   Did you spell the word right?
   If not, go back to step 1.

Spelling Tip

When a word ends with a silent **e**, drop the final **e** when adding a suffix that starts with a vowel.

resid**e** + ent = resid**e**nt

When a word ends with a consonant and **y**, change the **y** to **i** before adding a suffix.

dizz**y** + ness = dizz**i**ness

Scrambled Words

Unscramble each spelling word below.

1. selsdobun _____
2. tendendasc _____
3. selghtiss _____
4. tonpucac _____
5. caannuitcqae _____
6. eszinzids _____
7. sistetnrep _____
8. lentlcexe _____
9. verlencsse _____
10. ragesedrls _____

11. sesrlets _____
12. yanancneo _____
13. dinretse _____
14. feenccoern _____
15. petinsmes _____
16. recnreuocc _____
17. rocesdreontnp _____
18. freenerce _____
19. teandantt _____
20. streubidanc _____

To Parents or Helpers:

Using the Word Study Steps above as your child comes across any new words will help him or her spell words effectively. Review the steps as you both go over this week's spelling words.

Go over the Spelling Tip with your child. Help your child find other examples of words which change y to i and drop the final e. Help your child complete the Spelling Activity by unscrambling each set of letters above.

Words with Suffixes

excellent	conference	cleverness	sightless	boundless
attendant	resident	reference	descendant	emptiness
restless	annoyance	acquaintance	dizziness	correspondent
disturbance	occupant	persistent	occurrence	regardless

Sort each spelling word according to the suffix which it contains. Write the words with the following suffixes:

-ness

1. _____

2. _____

3. _____

-less

4. _____

5. _____

6. _____

7. _____

-ant

8. _____

9. _____

10. _____

-ent

11. _____

12. _____

13. _____

14. _____

-ance

15. _____

16. _____

17. _____

-ence

18. _____

19. _____

20. _____

Words with Suffixes

excellent	conference	cleverness	sightless	boundless
attendant	resident	reference	descendant	emptiness
restless	annoyance	acquaintance	dizziness	correspondent
disturbance	occupant	persistent	occurrence	regardless

Synonyms and Antonyms

Write the spelling word which is a synonym (S) or antonym (A).

1. order (A) _____

2. offspring (S) _____

3. balance (A) _____

4. nuisance (S) _____

5. stranger (A) _____

6. superior (S) _____

7. blind (S) _____

8. restful (A) _____

9. meeting (S) _____

10. stupidity (A) _____

11. enduring (S) _____

12. limited (A) _____

Word Meanings: Analogies

An **analogy** compares the relationship between two pairs of words. Fill in the spelling word that best completes each analogy below.

13. *Boss* is to *employer* as *servant* is to _____

14. *Poem* is to *poet* as *letter* is to _____

15. *Everything* is to *fullness* as *nothing* is to _____

16. *Spoon* is to *utensil* as *dictionary* is to _____

17. *Own* is to *owner* as *occupy* is to _____

18. *Cautious* is to *careful* as *nevertheless* is to _____

19. *Outcome* is to *result* as *happening* is to _____

20. *Physician* is to *doctor* as *intern* is to _____

Challenge Extension: Write an updated version of an old fairytale using the Challenge Words.

Grade 6/Unit 5
Rumpelstiltskin's Daughter

`20`

Words with Suffixes

Proofreading Activity

There are six spelling mistakes in this paragraph. Circle the misspelled words. Write the words correctly on the lines below.

The miller claimed that his desendant could spin straw into gold. The king's

attendent heard the claim, and ran off to tell the king. The king arrived at the

miller's house and looked for the ocupant. Eventually the miller appeared,

showing anoyance at having been disturbed. The king demanded to know which

aquaintance of the miller could spin straw into gold. But the miller refused to tell

unless he was paid for the referrence. Finally, the king threw down a gold coin,

grabbed the miller's daughter, and took her away to the palace.

1. _____   3. _____   5. _____

2. _____   4. _____   6. _____

Writing Activity

Rewrite the ending to *Rumpelstiltskin's Daughter* or another fairy tale with which you are familiar. Use four spelling words in your writing.

_____

_____

_____

_____

Words with Suffixes

Look at the words in each set below. One word in each set is spelled correctly. Use a pencil to fill in the circle next to the correct word. Before you begin, look at the sample sets of words. Sample A has been done for you. Do Sample B by yourself. When you are sure you know what to do, you may go on with the rest of the page.

Sample A:
- (A) happeyness
- (B) happyness
- (C) happieness
- (D) happiness ●

Sample B:
- (E) depandent
- (F) dependent
- (G) dapendant
- (H) dapendent

1.
- (A) disturbence
- (B) disturbance
- (C) distirbence
- (D) distirbance

2.
- (E) persistent
- (F) persistant
- (G) persisstent
- (H) persisstant

3.
- (A) regardliss
- (B) regardles
- (C) regardless
- (D) ragardless

4.
- (E) cleverness
- (F) clevverness
- (G) clevirness
- (H) clevvirness

5.
- (A) bondless
- (B) bowndless
- (C) boundless
- (D) bownddless

6.
- (E) annoyence
- (F) annoyance
- (G) anoyence
- (H) anoyance

7.
- (A) resident
- (B) residant
- (C) rezident
- (D) rezidant

8.
- (E) exellent
- (F) exellant
- (G) excellant
- (H) excellent

9.
- (A) disiness
- (B) diziness
- (C) dissiness
- (D) dizziness

10.
- (E) ocupant
- (F) occupant
- (G) ocupent
- (H) occupent

11.
- (A) emptyness
- (B) emptiness
- (C) emptynes
- (D) emptines

12.
- (E) atendent
- (F) atendant
- (G) attendent
- (H) attendant

13.
- (A) siteliss
- (B) siteles
- (C) sightless
- (D) sightles

14.
- (E) reference
- (F) refference
- (G) refrence
- (H) reffrence

15.
- (A) correspondent
- (B) corrispondent
- (C) correspondant
- (D) corrispondant

16.
- (E) aquaintence
- (F) acquaintance
- (G) acquaintence
- (H) aquaintance

17.
- (A) resstless
- (B) restless
- (C) restliss
- (D) resstliss

18.
- (E) accurence
- (F) accurance
- (G) occurrence
- (H) occurance

19.
- (A) confrence
- (B) conference
- (C) confrenss
- (D) conferenss

20.
- (E) desendant
- (F) desendent
- (G) descendant
- (H) descendint

Words from Math

Pretest Directions

Fold back the paper along the dotted line. Use the blanks to write each word as it is read aloud. When you finish the test, unfold the paper. Use the list at the right to correct any spelling mistakes. Practice the words you missed for the Posttest.

To Parents

Here are the results of your child's weekly spelling Pretest. You can help your child study for the Posttest by following these simple steps for each word on the word list:

1. Read the word to your child.

2. Have your child write the word, saying each letter as it is written.

3. Say each letter of the word as your child checks the spelling.

4. If a mistake has been made, have your child read each letter of the correctly spelled word aloud, and then repeat steps 1–3.

1. _____
2. _____
3. _____
4. _____
5. _____
6. _____
7. _____
8. _____
9. _____
10. _____
11. _____
12. _____
13. _____
14. _____
15. _____
16. _____
17. _____
18. _____
19. _____
20. _____

1. interest
2. borrow
3. division
4. percent
5. addition
6. fraction
7. metric
8. positive
9. calculate
10. customary
11. predict
12. deposit
13. discount
14. negative
15. probable
16. decimal
17. tally
18. dividend
19. subtraction
20. statistics

Challenge Words

_____
_____
_____
_____
_____

bartering
currency
fee
loan
automated

Words from Math

Using the Word Study Steps

1. LOOK at the word.
2. SAY the word aloud.
3. STUDY the letters in the word.
4. WRITE the word.
5. CHECK the word.

    Did you spell the word right?
    If not, go back to step 1.

Spelling Tip

Look for word chunks that help you remember the spelling. Sometimes there may be smaller words in a longer word that will help you to spell it.

per cent   cus to mar y

dis count

Rhyme Time!

Circle the word that rhymes with each spelling word on the left.

1. division   decision   devotion   divide

2. discount   discuss   among   amount

3. fraction   picture   traction   react

4. calculate   combination   treatment   demonstrate

5. predict   prepare   evict   select

6. tally   rally   tall   trail

7. borrow   hello   sorrow   bore

8. percent   token   absent   person

9. metric   hectic   metal   price

10. addition   added   admission   adding

To Parents or Helpers:

Using the Word Study Steps above as your child comes across any new words will help him or her spell words effectively. Review the steps as you both go over this week's spelling words.

Go over the Spelling Tip with your child. Help him or her divide the longer spelling words into word chunks.

Help your child complete the Spelling Activity by circling the rhyming words.

Words from Math

interest	addition	calculate	discount	tally
borrow	fraction	customary	negative	dividend
division	metric	predict	probable	subtraction
percent	positive	deposit	decimal	statistics

Use a dictionary to find the syllable that is stressed. Then sort the spelling words by the type of short vowel sound in the stressed syllable.

Short _a_

1. _____
2. _____
3. _____
4. _____

Short _i_

5. _____
6. _____
7. _____
8. _____
9. _____
10. _____
11. _____

Short _u_

12. _____

Short _e_

13. _____
14. _____
15. _____
16. _____

Short _o_

17. _____
18. _____
19. _____
20. _____

Words from Math

interest	addition	calculate	discount	tally
borrow	fraction	customary	negative	dividend
division	metric	predict	probable	subtraction
percent	positive	deposit	decimal	statistics

Matching Symbols

Write the letter of the mathematical example in the right column which matches the spelling word on the left.

1. _____	addition	**a.** $360 \div 4 = 90$
2. _____	fraction	**b.** -1
3. _____	negative	**c.** 2.44
4. _____	division	**d.** $47 - 23 = 24$
5. _____	decimal	**e.** 1/2
6. _____	subtraction	**f.** 15%
7. _____	percent	**g.** $2 + 7 = 9$
8. _____	positive	**h.** $+4$

Analogies

An analogy compares the relationship between two pairs of words. Fill in the spelling word that best completes each analogy.

9. *Take* is to *give* as *lend* is to _____

10. *Yard* is to *English* as *meter* is to _____

11. *Habit* is to *habitual* as *custom* is to _____

12. *Subtract* is to *remove* as *add* is to _____

13. *Mailbox* is to *letter* as *savings* is to _____

14. *Computer* is to *compute* as *calculator* is to _____

15. *Normal* is to *usual* as *likely* is to _____

Challenge Extension: Write a definition for each challenge word. Then write a sentence using each challenge word.

Words from Math

Proofreading Activity
There are six spelling mistakes in the paragraph below. Circle the misspelled words.
Write the words correctly on the lines below.

A long time ago, it was custumary for people to trade what they had to get what
they wanted. People might taly their pottery bowls and trade them for some food.
Depending on the harvest, a farmer might offer a diskount when there was an
abundance of food, or perhaps borow from other traders when supplies were low.
It is probbable, though, that people learned how to pradict what supplies would be
needed and in what quantity throughout the year.

1. _____   3. _____   5. _____

2. _____   4. _____   6. _____

Writing Activity
What activities make math class more fun and interesting? Write a letter to your math
teacher making some suggestions. Use four spelling words in your letter.

_____
_____
_____
_____

Words from Math

Look at the words in each set below. One word in each set is spelled correctly. Use a pencil to fill in the circle next to the correct word. Before you begin, look at the sample sets of words. Sample A has been done for you. Do Sample B by yourself. When you are sure you know what to do, you may go on with the rest of the page.

Sample A:

- (A) multiplie
- (B) multipli
- (C) multipliy
- (D) **multiply**

Sample B:

- (E) tryangle
- (F) triangel
- (G) triangle
- (H) tryangel

1.
- (A) posative
- (B) positive
- (C) posativ
- (D) positiv

2.
- (E) dividind
- (F) dividend
- (G) divvidend
- (H) divvidind

3.
- (A) neggative
- (B) negativve
- (C) negative
- (D) negativ

4.
- (E) fraction
- (F) fracion
- (G) fraccion
- (H) fracsion

5.
- (A) probabble
- (B) probable
- (C) prababl
- (D) prabable

6.
- (E) persent
- (F) pircent
- (G) purcent
- (H) percent

7.
- (A) subtraction
- (B) subractun
- (C) subtracktion
- (D) sibtraction

8.
- (E) taly
- (F) tally
- (G) tallie
- (H) talie

9.
- (A) adition
- (B) addation
- (C) addition
- (D) aditon

10.
- (E) borrow
- (F) borro
- (G) borow
- (H) boro

11.
- (A) intrest
- (B) intresst
- (C) interest
- (D) interesst

12.
- (E) desimal
- (F) decimal
- (G) dessimal
- (H) descima

13.
- (A) depasit
- (B) depossit
- (C) depozit
- (D) deposit

14.
- (E) metric
- (F) mettric
- (G) metrick
- (H) mettrick

15.
- (A) calculate
- (B) calckulate
- (C) calcoolate
- (D) calculat

16.
- (E) divition
- (F) division
- (G) divicion
- (H) divission

17.
- (A) pridict
- (B) predickt
- (C) predick
- (D) predict

18.
- (E) discount
- (F) diskount
- (G) discownt
- (H) diskownt

19.
- (A) customary
- (B) custamary
- (C) custamarry
- (D) customarry

20.
- (E) statisstics
- (F) stattistics
- (G) statistics
- (H) stattisstics

Grade 6/Unit 5 Review Test

Read each sentence. If an underlined word is spelled wrong, fill in the circle that goes with that word. If no word is spelled wrong, fill in the circle below NONE.

Read Sample A and do Sample B.

A. This <u>weekind</u> we had a <u>celebration</u> for our <u>sister-in-law</u>.
    A   B   C

NONE
A. Ⓐ   Ⓑ   Ⓒ   Ⓓ

B. The <u>babysiter</u> had <u>endless</u> <u>patience</u>.
         E   F   G

NONE
B. Ⓔ   Ⓕ   Ⓖ   Ⓗ

1. The <u>crosscountry</u> skier had the most <u>boundless</u> energy <u>imaginable</u>.
           A   B   C

NONE
1. Ⓐ   Ⓑ   Ⓒ   Ⓓ

2. "This is not <u>permissible</u> for our <u>new-born</u> pet <u>dove</u>," she said.
               E   F   G

NONE
2. Ⓔ   Ⓕ   Ⓖ   Ⓗ

3. My <u>acquaintance</u> liked <u>cerial</u> shows without <u>interruption</u>.
       A   B   C

NONE
3. Ⓐ   Ⓑ   Ⓒ   Ⓓ

4. After the final <u>talley</u> there was <u>dizziness</u> and <u>perspiration</u>.
                 E   F   G

NONE
4. Ⓔ   Ⓕ   Ⓖ   Ⓗ

5. She was <u>persistent</u> in her effort to <u>hier</u> a <u>self-reliant</u> worker.
          A   B   C

NONE
5. Ⓐ   Ⓑ   Ⓒ   Ⓓ

6. In a <u>higher</u> grade, we use the <u>question</u> mark and <u>decimal</u> point.
      E   F   G

NONE
6. Ⓔ   Ⓕ   Ⓖ   Ⓗ

7. It is a usual <u>ocurrence</u> to eat <u>cereal</u> in a <u>bathrobe</u>.
             A   B   C

NONE
7. Ⓐ   Ⓑ   Ⓒ   Ⓓ

8. It is not <u>customary</u> to have an <u>interruption</u> in the <u>divident</u>.
         E   F   G

NONE
8. Ⓔ   Ⓕ   Ⓖ   Ⓗ

9. A <u>cross-country</u> race without <u>perspiration</u> is not <u>imagineable</u>.
      A   B   C

NONE
9. Ⓐ   Ⓑ   Ⓒ   Ⓓ

10. The <u>persistant</u> writers created a <u>boundless</u> <u>serial</u> program.
      E   F   G

NONE
10. Ⓔ   Ⓕ   Ⓖ   Ⓗ

Go on

Grade 6/Unit 5 Review Test

11. Is it <u>permisible</u> to have this <u>festivity</u> as a regular <u>occurrence</u>? 11. Ⓐ Ⓑ Ⓒ Ⓓ NONE
     A   B   C

12. I'll <u>hire</u> someone <u>self-reliant</u> to take care of the <u>newborn</u>. 12. Ⓔ Ⓕ Ⓖ Ⓗ NONE
     E   F   G

13. It's not <u>customery</u> nor <u>permissible</u> to omit a <u>question mark</u>. 13. Ⓐ Ⓑ Ⓒ Ⓓ NONE
       A   B   C

14. The <u>persistent</u> student learned to <u>tally</u> <u>decimel</u> numbers. 14. Ⓔ Ⓕ Ⓖ Ⓗ NONE
     E   F G

15. Is your <u>acquaintance</u> <u>self reliant</u> enough to go <u>cross-country</u>? 15. Ⓐ Ⓑ Ⓒ Ⓓ NONE
     A   B   C

16. During the <u>festivity</u> we gave the <u>newborn</u> a <u>bathrob</u>. 16. Ⓔ Ⓕ Ⓖ Ⓗ NONE
       E   F   G

17. In a state of <u>diziness</u> she <u>dove</u> off the <u>higher</u> cliff. 17. Ⓐ Ⓑ Ⓒ Ⓓ NONE
       A   B   C

18. The <u>occurrence</u> included a <u>tally</u> of raisins in the <u>sereal</u>. 18. Ⓔ Ⓕ Ⓖ Ⓗ NONE
     E   F   G

19. It is <u>customary</u> for the <u>festivitey</u> to go without <u>interruption</u>. 19. Ⓐ Ⓑ Ⓒ Ⓓ NONE
     A   B   C

20. My <u>aquaintance</u> will help you <u>tally</u> your <u>dividend</u> earnings. 20. Ⓔ Ⓕ Ⓖ Ⓗ NONE
     E   F   G

21. I put a <u>deposit</u> on the fanciest <u>bathrobe</u> <u>imaginable</u>. 21. Ⓐ Ⓑ Ⓒ Ⓓ NONE
     A   B C

22. I was <u>persistent</u> that the <u>dividend</u> should be no <u>higher</u>. 22. Ⓔ Ⓕ Ⓖ Ⓗ NONE
     E   F   G

23. It's <u>imaginable</u> that the <u>serial</u> will stop during the <u>festividy</u>. 23. Ⓐ Ⓑ Ⓒ Ⓓ NONE
     A   B   C

24. It is not <u>customary</u> to have a <u>decimal</u> point in your <u>deposet</u>. 24. Ⓔ Ⓕ Ⓖ Ⓗ NONE
     E   F   G

25. The <u>dizziness</u> caused <u>persperation</u> at the <u>higher</u> peaks. 25. Ⓐ Ⓑ Ⓒ Ⓓ NONE
     A   B   C

Words with Prefixes

Pretest Directions

Fold back the paper along the dotted line. Use the blanks to write each word as it is read aloud. When you finish the test, unfold the paper. Use the list at the right to correct any spelling mistakes. Practice the words you missed for the Posttest.

To Parents

Here are the results of your child's weekly spelling Pretest. You can help your child study for the Posttest by following these simple steps for each word on the word list:

1. Read the word to your child.

2. Have your child write the word, saying each letter as it is written.

3. Say each letter of the word as your child checks the spelling.

4. If a mistake has been made, have your child read each letter of the correctly spelled word aloud, and then repeat steps 1–3.

1. _____ 1. discourage
2. _____ 2. unfairness
3. _____ 3. mislead
4. _____ 4. informal
5. _____ 5. unjustly
6. _____ 6. immature
7. _____ 7. dethroned
8. _____ 8. discontinue
9. _____ 9. misjudge
10. _____ 10. indirect
11. _____ 11. impolite
12. _____ 12. unpopular
13. _____ 13. improper
14. _____ 14. inequality
15. _____ 15. discontent
16. _____ 16. decipher
17. _____ 17. immovable
18. _____ 18. unnecessary
19. _____ 19. inseparable
20. _____ 20. misbehave

Challenge Words

_____ capable

_____ counselor

_____ equator

_____ nimbly

_____ stubbornness

Name _____ Date _____ **Spelling**

Words with Prefixes

Using the Word Study Steps

1. LOOK at the word
2. SAY the word aloud.
3. STUDY the letters in the word.
4. WRITE the word.
5. CHECK the word.

   Did you spell the word right?
   If not, go back to step 1.

Related Words

Write the spelling word which is related to each word below.

1. courage _____
2. fairness_____
3. lead _____
4. formal _____
5. justly _____
6. mature _____
7. throned _____
8. continue _____
9. judge _____
10. direct _____

11. polite _____
12. popular _____
13. proper _____
14. equality _____
15. content _____
16. cipher _____
17. movable _____
18. necessary _____
19. separable _____
20. behave _____

Words with Prefixes

discourage	unjustly	misjudge	improper	immovable
unfairness	immature	indirect	inequality	unnecessary
mislead	dethroned	impolite	discontent	inseparable
informal	discontinue	unpopular	decipher	misbehave

Prefix Patterns

Sort each spelling word according to the prefix it contains. Write the spelling words with the following prefixes:

un

1. _____

2. _____

3. _____

4. _____

de

5. _____

6. _____

in

7. _____

8. _____

9. _____

10. _____

im

11. _____

12. _____

13. _____

14. _____

dis

15. _____

16. _____

17. _____

mis

18. _____

19. _____

20. _____

Words with Prefixes

discourage	unjustly	misjudge	improper	immovable
unfairness	immature	indirect	inequality	unnecessary
mislead	dethroned	impolite	discontent	inseparable
informal	discontinue	unpopular	decipher	misbehave

Similar Meanings

Write the spelling word which has the same or similar meaning as each word or words below.

1. dishearten _____

2. unjustness _____

3. deceive _____

4. casual _____

5. stop _____

6. roundabout _____

7. rude _____

8. not liked _____

9. inappropriate _____

10. needless _____

11. translate _____

12. stationary _____

Fill-In's

Fill in the missing blanks below with the appropriate spelling word.

1. To be _____ is to be foolish or infantile.

2. He acted _____ when he only punished one of the criminals.

3. If you _____ someone's character, you judge them unfairly.

4. There is great _____ between the rich and poor.

5. The twins did everything together; they were _____.

6. If you _____, you may get punished.

7. The people voted to have the king _____.

8. There was much _____ among the team after they lost.

Challenge Extension: Have students use each Challenge Word in a sentence.

Grade 6/Unit 6
Mandela

20

Words with Prefixes

Proofreading Activity

There are six spelling mistakes in the paragraph below. Circle each misspelled word. Write the words correctly on the lines below.

Mandela was still a child when he learned about standing firm on principle. His father was disthroned when he refused to appear before an English magistrate. Mandela's family would rather be poor than be treated injustly. All his life, Mandela objected to any type of unfairnes. In particular, he fought against racial unequality. Although his activities were unpopuler with white rulers, he did not let this descourage him.

1. _____   3. _____   5. _____

2. _____   4. _____   6. _____

Writing Activity

Write a letter to a friend describing what you have learned about Mandela and his accomplishments. Use four spelling words in your writing.

_____

_____

_____

_____

Words with Prefixes

Look at the words in each set below. One word in each set is spelled correctly. Use a pencil to fill in the circle next to the correct word. Before you begin, look at the sample sets of words. Sample A has been done for you. Do Sample B by yourself. When you are sure you know what to do, you may go on with the rest of the page.

Sample A:
- (A) undonne
- (B) unndone
- (C) indone
- ● **(D) undone**

Sample B:
- (E) inabbility
- (F) unability
- (G) inability
- (H) innability

1. (A) unpolite
   (B) dispolite
   (C) inpolite
   (D) impolite

2. (E) imdirect
   (F) indirect
   (G) undirect
   (H) disdirect

3. (A) unpopular
   (B) inpopular
   (C) impopular
   (D) unpopuler

4. (E) disjudge
   (F) disjuge
   (G) misjudge
   (H) misjuge

5. (A) misproper
   (B) inproper
   (C) improper
   (D) unproper

6. (E) discontinue
   (F) miscontinue
   (G) decontinue
   (H) decuntinue

7. (A) disbehave
   (B) disbehaive
   (C) misbehave
   (D) misbehaive

8. (E) misleed
   (F) missleed
   (G) misslead
   (H) mislead

9. (A) imovable
   (B) immovable
   (C) inmovable
   (D) unmovable

10. (E) inmature
    (F) unmature
    (G) immature
    (H) imature

11. (A) descorage
    (B) decourage
    (C) discorage
    (D) discourage

12. (E) discontent
    (F) descontent
    (G) descantent
    (H) discantent

13. (A) disthroned
    (B) unthroned
    (C) dethroned
    (D) dethronned

14. (E) unequality
    (F) imequality
    (G) disequality
    (H) inequality

15. (A) injustly
    (B) unjustly
    (C) injustley
    (D) unjustley

16. (E) dicipher
    (F) discipher
    (G) decipher
    (H) decigher

17. (A) unformal
    (B) imformle
    (C) informle
    (D) informal

18. (E) unecessary
    (F) unnecessary
    (G) innecesary
    (H) innecessary

19. (A) iunfairness
    (B) infairness
    (C) unfairnes
    (D) unfairness

20. (E) unseparable
    (F) inseparable
    (G) unseparible
    (H) inseparible

Words from Foreign Languages

Pretest Directions

Fold back the paper along the dotted line. Use the blanks to write each word as it is read aloud. When you finish the test, unfold the paper. Use the list at the right to correct any spelling mistakes. Practice the words you missed for the Posttest.

To Parents

Here are the results of your child's weekly spelling Pretest. You can help your child study for the Posttest by following these simple steps for each word on the word list:

1. Read the word to your child.

2. Have your child write the word, saying each letter as it is written.

3. Say each letter of the word as your child checks the spelling.

4. If a mistake has been made, have your child read each letter of the correctly spelled word aloud, and then repeat steps 1–3.

1. _____	1. garage
2. _____	2. coyote
3. _____	3. spaghetti
4. _____	4. ravine
5. _____	5. ballet
6. _____	6. chutes
7. _____	7. tempo
8. _____	8. macaroni
9. _____	9. chandelier
10. _____	10. routine
11. _____	11. adobe
12. _____	12. mustache
13. _____	13. bouquet
14. _____	14. sierra
15. _____	15. limousine
16. _____	16. mirage
17. _____	17. beret
18. _____	18. siesta
19. _____	19. cello
20. _____	20. chagrined

Challenge Words

_____	concealed
_____	darning
_____	poring
_____	rebellious
_____	sauntered

Words from Foreign Languages

Using the Word Study Steps

1. LOOK at the word.
2. SAY the word aloud.
3. STUDY the letters in the word.
4. WRITE the word.
5. CHECK the word.
   Did you spell the word right?
   If not, go back to step 1.

Spelling Tip

Use a secret pronunciation of your own to help you spell some hard words.

spaghetti /spag **h**et ī/

mirage /mir a **g**ə/

Finish the Word

Fill in the missing blanks below to form spelling words.

1. gara _____ _____

2. coy _____ te

3. spaghett _____

4. rav _____ n _____

5. ball _____ _____

6. _____ _____ utes

7. temp _____

8. macaron _____

9. _____ _____ andelier

10. rout _____ n _____

11. ad _____ be

12. musta _____ _____ e

13. bouq _____ _____ _____

14. s _____ erra

15. limous _____ n _____

16. mira _____ _____

17. ber _____ _____

18. s _____ esta

19. cell _____

20. _____ _____ agrined

To Parents or Helpers:

Using the Word Study Steps above as the student comes across any new words will help him or her spell words effectively. Review the steps as you both go over this week's spelling words.

Go over the Spelling Tip with the student. Help your child come up with secret pronunciations for hard words.

Help the student complete the spelling activity by filling in the missing letters.

Name_____ Date_____

Words from Foreign Languages

garage	ballet	chandelier	bouquet	beret
coyote	chutes	routine	sierra	siesta
spaghetti	tempo	adobe	limousine	cello
ravine	macaroni	mustache	mirage	chagrined

Pattern Power!

Sort each spelling word by finding the sound and spelling pattern to which it belongs. Write the words with the following patterns on the lines below.

/ō/ spelled o

1. _____

2. _____

3. _____

4. _____

/ē/ spelled i

5. _____

6. _____

7. _____

8. _____

/ē/ spelled i-e

9. _____

10. _____

11. _____

/ā/ spelled et

12. _____

13. _____

14. _____

/sh/ spelled ch

15. _____

16. _____

17. _____

18. _____

/zh/ spelled ge

19. _____

20. _____

Words from Foreign Languages

garage	ballet	chandelier	bouquet	beret
coyote	chutes	routine	sierra	siesta
spaghetti	tempo	adobe	limousine	cello
ravine	macaroni	mustache	mirage	chagrined

Word Meanings

Add the spelling word that is related in meaning to each of the words below.

1. plaster _____   **9.** shed _____

2. rhythm _____   **10.** dance _____

3. nap _____   **11.** hat _____

4. wolf _____   **12.** light _____

5. violin _____   **13.** ashamed _____

6. sedan _____   **14.** illusion _____

7. gully _____   **15.** mountain _____

8. beard _____   **16.** slides _____

Sentence Completion

Fill in the blank with the appropriate spelling word.

1. My favorite meal is _____ and cheese.

2. He bought me a _____ of flowers.

3. As part of her bedtime _____, she brushes her teeth.

4. We ate a large plate of _____ and meatballs.

Words from Foreign Languages

Proofreading Activity

There are six spelling mistakes in the paragraph below. Circle each misspelled word.
Write the words correctly on the lines below.

Cleaning Flicka's wounds had become a daily rootine. Today Kennie could not
find her. He was walking past the adobee garauge when he heard a cyote howling
from the siera. Kennie continued walking and found Flicka in a stream that ran
along the bottom of the raveen. The stream was washing the infection from her
wounds and the fever from her body.

1. _____ 3. _____ 5. _____

2. _____ 4. _____ 6. _____

Writing Activity

Write about an experience you may have had trying to earn someone's trust. Use
four spelling words.

_____

_____

_____

_____

Words from Foreign Languages

Look at the words in each set below. One word in each set is spelled correctly. Use a pencil to fill in the circle next to the correct word. Before you begin, look at the sample sets of words. Sample A has been done for you. Do Sample B by yourself. When you are sure you know what to do, you may go on with the rest of the page.

Sample A:
- (A) passta
- (B) pasda
- (C) pastta
- (D) pasta ●

Sample B:
- (E) mashine
- (F) machine
- (G) machene
- (H) mashene

1. (A) ballay
   (B) balay
   (C) ballet
   (D) balet

2. (E) seirra
   (F) sierra
   (G) siarra
   (H) siara

3. (A) coyote
   (B) cyote
   (C) coyoty
   (D) cyoty

4. (E) shandalier
   (F) chandalier
   (G) shandelier
   (H) chandelier

5. (A) cello
   (B) chello
   (C) celo
   (D) chelo

6. (E) mirrage
   (F) mirrase
   (G) mirage
   (H) mirase

7. (A) shootes
   (B) chootes
   (C) chutes
   (D) choots

8. (E) boquet
   (F) bouquet
   (G) bouquay
   (H) boquay

9. (A) spagetti
   (B) spaghetti
   (C) spagheti
   (D) spageti

10. (E) beret
    (F) berret
    (G) baray
    (H) barray

11. (A) gorage
    (B) goradge
    (C) garage
    (D) garadge

12. (E) limusine
    (F) limosine
    (G) limouseen
    (H) limousine

13. (A) adoby
    (B) adobee
    (C) adobe
    (D) addobe

14. (E) ravine
    (F) ravien
    (G) raveen
    (H) ravean

15. (A) shagrined
    (B) chagrined
    (C) shugrined
    (D) chugrined

16. (E) temmpo
    (F) temppo
    (G) tempow
    (H) tempo

17. (A) seista
    (B) siesta
    (C) syesta
    (D) siessta

18. (E) macaroni
    (F) maceroni
    (G) macarony
    (H) macerony

19. (A) mustashe
    (B) mustash
    (C) mustach
    (D) mustache

20. (E) rountine
    (F) routine
    (G) rootine
    (H) routeen

Words with Latin Roots

Pretest Directions

Fold back the paper along the dotted line. Use the blanks to write each word as it is read aloud. When you finish the test, unfold the paper. Use the list at the right to correct any spelling mistakes. Practice the words you missed for the Posttest.

To Parents

Here are the results of your child's weekly spelling Pretest. You can help your child study for the Posttest by following these simple steps for each word on the word list:

1. Read the word to your child.

2. Have your child write the word, saying each letter as it is written.

3. Say each letter of the word as your child checks the spelling.

4. If a mistake has been made, have your child read each letter of the correctly spelled word aloud, and then repeat steps 1–3.

#		#	Word
1.	_____	1.	depended
2.	_____	2.	position
3.	_____	3.	progress
4.	_____	4.	procession
5.	_____	5.	transportation
6.	_____	6.	suspense
7.	_____	7.	gradual
8.	_____	8.	specimens
9.	_____	9.	porter
10.	_____	10.	inspect
11.	_____	11.	graduate
12.	_____	12.	posture
13.	_____	13.	precede
14.	_____	14.	spectator
15.	_____	15.	portable
16.	_____	16.	postpone
17.	_____	17.	pendulum
18.	_____	18.	recede
19.	_____	19.	aggressive
20.	_____	20.	dispense

Challenge Words

_____ botanists

_____ plundered

_____ surveyors

_____ tutor

_____ worthwhile

Name_____ Date_____

Words with Latin Roots

Using the Word Study Steps

1. LOOK at the word.
2. SAY the word aloud.
3. STUDY the letters in the word.
4. WRITE the word.
5. CHECK the word.

   Did you spell the word right?
   If not, go back to step 1.

> **Spelling Tip**
>
> Learning common Latin roots, their spellings, and their meanings, will help you remember both the meanings and the spellings of the words containing them.
>
> **vis** = see
> **vis**ible, **vis**ion, ad**vis**e
> **script** = write
> in**script**ion, sub**script**ion

Scrambled Words

Unscramble each group of letters below to form spelling words.

1. rotrep _____
2. nessesup _____
3. tisipono _____
4. sempinecs _____
5. sropneciso _____
6. tecspin_____
7. sorgreps _____
8. tonnitropartas _____
9. pededned_____
10. dalarug _____

11. poposten _____
12. decrepe _____
13. sragvigese _____
14. blotaper _____
15. taudegar _____
16. deerec _____
17. ludunemp _____
18. retspocta _____
19. nepsidse _____
20. topurse _____

To Parents or Helpers:

Using the Word Study Steps above as the student comes across any new words will help him or her spell words effectively. Review the steps as you both go over this week's spelling words.

Go over the Spelling Tip with the student. Ask for students to think of other words from Latin roots, such as **description** or **envision**.

Help your child complete the Spelling Activity by unscrambling the words.

Words with Latin Roots

depended	transportation	porter	precede	pendulum
position	suspense	inspect	spectator	recede
progress	gradual	graduate	portable	aggressive
procession	specimens	posture	postpone	dispense

Root Power

Sort each spelling word according to the Latin root it contains. Write the words with the following Latin roots:

port

1. _____
2. _____
3. _____

spec

4. _____
5. _____
6. _____

grad/gress

7. _____
8. _____
9. _____
10. _____

pon/pos

11. _____
12. _____
13. _____

cede/ceed/cess

14. _____
15. _____
16. _____

pend/pens

17. _____
18. _____
19. _____
20. _____

Words with Latin Roots

depended	transportation	porter	precede	pendulum
position	suspense	inspect	spectator	recede
progress	gradual	graduate	portable	aggressive
procession	specimens	posture	postpone	dispense

Definitions
Match each of the definitions below with one of the spelling words.

1. a person employed to carry baggage _____

2. to look at closely and critically _____

3. to move back or away _____

4. the place occupied by a person or thing _____

5. moving, changing, or happening slowly _____

6. to give or deal out in portions _____

7. able to be carried _____

8. one who watches _____

9. to put off to a later time _____

10. forward movement _____

11. to go before _____

12. state of being undecided or in doubt _____

Synonyms
Write the spelling word which comes closest in meaning to each word below.

13. relied _____   **16.** delay _____

14. examples _____   **17.** pushy _____

15. transit _____   **18.** progression _____

Challenge Extension: Have students use each
Challenge Word in a sentence. Suggest they use
176 dictionaries to verify meanings.

Grade 6/Unit 6
Alexander the Great | 18 |

Words with Latin Roots

Proofreading Activity

There are six spelling mistakes in the paragraph below. Circle each misspelled word. Write the words correctly on the lines below.

Alexander's mother dipended on a tutor to educate her son. The tutor wanted Alexander to be tough and live simply. He would inspict Alexander's belongings for expensive possessions. The posicion of tutor was later taken by Aristotle, a gradduate of Plato's Academy. Alexander made excellent progres as Aristotle's pupil. Then, Alexander began his military training, launching an agressive attack when he was only eighteen.

1. _____   3. _____   5. _____

2. _____   4. _____   6. _____

Writing Activity

Write a few lines a biographer might write about Alexander. Use at least four spelling words.

_____

_____

_____

_____

Words with Latin Roots

Look at the words in each set below. One word in each set is spelled correctly. Use a pencil to fill in the circle next to the correct word. Before you begin, look at the sample sets of words. Sample A has been done for you. Do Sample B by yourself. When you are sure you know what to do, you may go on with the rest of the page.

Sample A:
- Ⓐ resspeckt
- Ⓑ respeckt
- ● respect
- Ⓓ rispect

Sample B:
- Ⓔ reporrt
- Ⓕ raport
- Ⓖ reporte
- Ⓗ report

1.
- Ⓐ portter
- Ⓑ porter
- Ⓒ proter
- Ⓓ portor

2.
- Ⓔ specimens
- Ⓕ specimans
- Ⓖ speccimens
- Ⓗ spectimens

3.
- Ⓐ innspect
- Ⓑ inspeckt
- Ⓒ inspecht
- Ⓓ inspect

4.
- Ⓔ graduel
- Ⓕ gradual
- Ⓖ gardual
- Ⓗ garduel

5.
- Ⓐ gradduate
- Ⓑ gradduite
- Ⓒ graduate
- Ⓓ graduite

6.
- Ⓔ saspense
- Ⓕ suspense
- Ⓖ suspens
- Ⓗ suspennse

7.
- Ⓐ poschure
- Ⓑ postere
- Ⓒ pausture
- Ⓓ posture

8.
- Ⓔ transpertation
- Ⓕ transportation
- Ⓖ transpirtation
- Ⓗ transportacion

9.
- Ⓐ preceed
- Ⓑ perceed
- Ⓒ percede
- Ⓓ precede

10.
- Ⓔ depinded
- Ⓕ depended
- Ⓖ deepended
- Ⓗ depennded

11.
- Ⓐ spechtator
- Ⓑ spechtater
- Ⓒ spectator
- Ⓓ spectater

12.
- Ⓔ aggresive
- Ⓕ agresive
- Ⓖ aggressive
- Ⓗ agressive

13.
- Ⓐ portible
- Ⓑ porttible
- Ⓒ protable
- Ⓓ portable

14.
- Ⓔ despense
- Ⓕ dispense
- Ⓖ despanse
- Ⓗ dispanse

15.
- Ⓐ pasition
- Ⓑ pasicion
- Ⓒ position
- Ⓓ posicion

16.
- Ⓔ pendgalum
- Ⓕ pendalum
- Ⓖ pendgulum
- Ⓗ pendulum

17.
- Ⓐ procession
- Ⓑ procesion
- Ⓒ procescion
- Ⓓ porcession

18.
- Ⓔ postpoan
- Ⓕ postponne
- Ⓖ postpone
- Ⓗ postpon

19.
- Ⓐ praugress
- Ⓑ praugres
- Ⓒ progres
- Ⓓ progress

20.
- Ⓔ receed
- Ⓕ recead
- Ⓖ recede
- Ⓗ reccede

Words with Prefixes

Pretest Directions

Fold back the paper along the dotted line. Use the blanks to write each word as it is read aloud. When you finish the test, unfold the paper. Use the list at the right to correct any spelling mistakes. Practice the words you missed for the Posttest.

To Parents

Here are the results of your child's weekly spelling Pretest. You can help your child study for the Posttest by following these simple steps for each word on the word list:

1. Read the word to your child.

2. Have your child write the word, saying each letter as it is written.

3. Say each letter of the word as your child checks the spelling.

4. If a mistake has been made, have your child read each letter of the correctly spelled word aloud, and then repeat steps 1–3.

1. _____	1. exchanged
2. _____	2. project
3. _____	3. compete
4. _____	4. contain
5. _____	5. recover
6. _____	6. export
7. _____	7. compound
8. _____	8. contract
9. _____	9. recess
10. _____	10. proceed
11. _____	11. compress
12. _____	12. expand
13. _____	13. prospect
14. _____	14. commotion
15. _____	15. respect
16. _____	16. recite
17. _____	17. composition
18. _____	18. consonant
19. _____	19. consequence
20. _____	20. exhale

Challenge Words

_____ acquired

_____ enthusiastically

_____ hesitantly

_____ husky

_____ instinctively

Name_____ Date_____ **Spelling**

Words with Prefixes

Using the Word Study Steps

1. LOOK at the word
2. SAY the word aloud.
3. STUDY the letters in the word.
4. WRITE the word.
5. CHECK the word.

   Did you spell the word right?
   If not, go back to step 1.

Spelling Tip
Learn the meanings and spellings of prefixes you often use in writing.
mis- (wrongly) misjudge, miscount
pre- (before) prearrange, preplan
un- (not) undecided, unamused

Write the spelling words which are related to the words or roots below.

1. changed _____
2. ject _____
3. pete _____
4. tain _____
5. cover _____
6. port _____
7. pound _____
8. tract _____
9. cess _____
10. ceed _____

11. press _____
12. pand _____
13. spect _____
14. motion _____
15. spect _____
16. cite _____
17. position _____
18. sonant _____
19. sequence _____
20. hale _____

To Parents or Helpers:

Using the Word Study Steps above as the student comes across any new words will help him or her spell words effectively. Review the steps as you both go over this week's spelling words.

Go over the Spelling Tip with the student. Have your child think of other words that begin with the prefixes listed, such as **unannounced** or **misplaced**.

Help your child complete the spelling activity by finding the spelling word related to each word or root.

Words with Prefixes

exchanged	recover	recess	prospect	composition
project	export	proceed	commotion	consonant
compete	compound	compress	respect	consequence
contain	contract	expand	recite	exhale

Pattern Power!

Sort each word according to the prefix which it contains. Write the list words that have the following prefixes:

re-

1. _____

2. _____

3. _____

4. _____

con-

5. _____

6. _____

7. _____

8. _____

pro-

9. _____

10. _____

11. _____

ex-

12. _____

13. _____

14. _____

15. _____

com-

16. _____

17. _____

18. _____

19. _____

20. _____

Words with Prefixes

exchanged	recover	recess	prospect	composition
project	export	proceed	commotion	consonant
compete	compound	compress	respect	consequence
contain	contract	expand	recite	exhale

Word Meanings

Write the spelling word that comes closest to the word pairs below.

1. throw + forward _____

2. hold + in _____

3. carry + out _____

4. draw + together _____

5. go + forward _____

6. spread + out _____

7. look + out _____

8. look + back _____

9. breathe + out _____

10. summon + back _____

Synonyms

Write the spelling word with the same or similar meaning as the word or words below.

1. traded _____

2. contest _____

3. regain _____

4. composite _____

5. intermission _____

6. condense _____

7. turmoil _____

8. ingredients _____

9. not a vowel _____

10. result _____

Challenge Extension: Have students write their own definitions for each Challenge Word. Then have them consult the dictionary and revise their definitions as needed.

182

Grade 6/Unit 6
The Circuit

20

Words with Prefixes

Proofreading Activity

There are six spelling mistakes in the paragraph below. Circle each misspelled word. Write the words correctly on the lines below.

Francisco was so excited about school he could hardly cantain himself. Yet he was nervous at the porspect of starting sixth grade in a new school. He could not compeet with students who had been attending class all year. To catch up, he studied at resess and lunch. The teacher helped with the words he did not know. Francisco needed to resite them a few times before he could remember them. Just as he started to make excellent progress, and his teacher suggested an exciting praject, his family packed up to move on again.

1. _____   3. _____   5. _____

2. _____   4. _____   6. _____

Writing Activity

Write some suggestions Francisco might need to see that he keeps up with other sixth graders when he is between schools. Use at least four spelling words.

_____

_____

_____

_____

Words with Prefixes

Look at the words in each set below. One word in each set is spelled correctly. Use a pencil to fill in the circle next to the correct word. Before you begin, look at the sample sets of words. Sample A has been done for you. Do Sample B by yourself. When you are sure you know what to do, you may go on with the rest of the page.

Sample A:

(A) compair
(B) compaire
(C) commpare
(D) compare ●

Sample B:

(E) repete
(F) repeat
(G) repeet
(H) rapeat

1. (A) prosceed
   (B) proceed
   (C) proscede
   (D) procede

2. (E) recess
   (F) resess
   (G) reces
   (H) reses

3. (A) compres
   (B) cummpres
   (C) compress
   (D) cumpress

4. (E) cauntract
   (F) conntract
   (G) comtract
   (H) contract

5. (A) ixpand
   (B) ecspand
   (C) expand
   (D) eccpand

6. (E) compound
   (F) caumpound
   (G) compownd
   (H) caumpownd

7. (A) porspect
   (B) prosspect
   (C) porsspect
   (D) prospect

8. (E) ixchanged
   (F) extianged
   (G) excianged
   (H) exchanged

9. (A) comotion
   (B) commotion
   (C) commocion
   (D) comocion

10. (E) consonant
    (F) consinant
    (G) consonint
    (H) consinint

11. (A) progect
    (B) prodgect
    (C) project
    (D) porject

12. (E) exale
    (F) exhale
    (G) exhail
    (H) exail

13. (A) cumpete
    (B) cumpeet
    (C) compete
    (D) compeet

14. (E) recite
    (F) rescite
    (G) resyte
    (H) recight

15. (A) conmposition
    (B) composition
    (C) conposition
    (D) compasition

16. (E) cuntain
    (F) contane
    (G) cuntane
    (H) contain

17. (A) respect
    (B) rescpect
    (C) resspect
    (D) recpect

18. (E) export
    (F) ecsport
    (G) ixport
    (H) exsport

19. (A) consiquence
    (B) consequence
    (C) consaquence
    (D) consequense

20. (E) recover
    (F) recuver
    (G) recovor
    (H) reecover

Words from Social Studies

Pretest Directions

Fold back the paper along the dotted line. Use the blanks to write each word as it is read aloud. When you finish the test, unfold the paper. Use the list at the right to correct any spelling mistakes. Practice the words you missed for the Posttest.

To Parents

Here are the results of your child's weekly spelling Pretest. You can help your child study for the Posttest by following these simple steps for each word on the word list:

1. Read the word to your child.

2. Have your child write the word, saying each letter as it is written.

3. Say each letter of the word as your child checks the spelling.

4. If a mistake has been made, have your child read each letter of the correctly spelled word aloud, and then repeat steps 1–3.

1. _____	1. pollution
2. _____	2. explanation
3. _____	3. extinct
4. _____	4. protest
5. _____	5. civilization
6. _____	6. disaster
7. _____	7. protective
8. _____	8. renew
9. _____	9. excess
10. _____	10. disappearance
11. _____	11. procedure
12. _____	12. revive
13. _____	13. generations
14. _____	14. excavate
15. _____	15. disprove
16. _____	16. evaporation
17. _____	17. replenish
18. _____	18. displaced
19. _____	19. irrigation
20. _____	20. starvation

Challenge Words

_____ ecological

_____ generators

_____ habitats

_____ reservoir

_____ temporary

Words from Social Studies

Using the Word Study Steps

1. LOOK at the word.
2. SAY the word aloud.
3. STUDY the letters in the word.
4. WRITE the word.
5. CHECK the word.

   Did you spell the word right?
   If not, go back to step 1.

Spelling Tip

Look for word chunks that help you remember the spelling of longer words.

disappearance =
   dis ap pear ance

explanation =
   ex pla na tion

Close Relations

Write the spelling word that is related to the word on the left.

1. pollute _____
2. explain _____
3. civilize _____
4. protect _____
5. test _____
6. new _____
7. appear _____

8. proceed _____
9. generate _____
10. prove _____
11. evaporate _____
12. place _____
13. irrigate _____
14. starve _____

Word Scramble

Write the spelling word formed by each group of letters below.

15. ttnciex _____
16. staidres _____
17. scexes _____

18. verevi _____
19. cextavea _____
20. shnirpeel _____

To Parents or Helpers:

Using the Word Study Steps above as your child comes across any new words will help him or her spell words effectively. Review the steps as you both go over this week's spelling words.

Go over the Spelling Tip with the student. Help your child break down longer words into word chunks.

Help your student complete the Spelling Activities.

Words from Social Studies

pollution	civilization	excess	generations	replenish
explanation	disaster	disappearance	excavate	displaced
extinct	protective	procedure	disprove	irrigation
protest	renew	revive	evaporation	starvation

Words with Prefixes

Sort the spelling words according to the prefix or suffix they contain. Write the words with the following prefixes:

re-

1. _____

2. _____

3. _____

dis-

4. _____

5. _____

6. _____

7. _____

ex-

8. _____

9. _____

10. _____

pro-

11. _____

12. _____

13. _____

Write the spelling words with the following suffixes:

-ion

14. _____

15. _____

16. _____

17. _____

-ation

18. _____

19. _____

20. _____

Words from Social Studies

pollution	civilization	excess	generations	replenish
explanation	disaster	disappearance	excavate	displaced
extinct	protective	procedure	disprove	irrigation
protest	renew	revive	evaporation	starvation

Word Meanings

Write the spelling word which has the same or similar meaning as each of the following words or phrases:

1. contamination _____

2. extinguished _____

3. complain _____

4. catastrophe _____

5. vanishing _____

6. keeping safe _____

7. restore _____

8. too much _____

9. course of action _____

10. resuscitate _____

11. dig out _____

12. refute _____

13. refill _____

14. replaced _____

Fill-In's

Use a spelling word to complete the following sentences.

15. He offered no _____ for his rude behavior that night.

16. The archaeologist discovered the remains of a lost _____.

17. This tradition has been in our family for _____.

18. Whole milk is changed to powdered milk through _____.

19. Crops can be grown in the desert if there is proper _____.

20. Due to the lack of food, many people died of _____.

Challenge Extension: Have students use each Challenge Word in a sentence. Suggest they use dictionaries to verify meanings.

Words from Social Studies

Proofreading Activity

There are six spelling mistakes in the paragraph below. Circle each misspelled word.
Write the words correctly on the lines below.

People in China must leave land their families have farmed for generacions.
They are being desplaced by construction of the world's largest dam. The dam
will use water power to supply as much electricity as fifteen coal-burning electric
plants. Burning coal creates more pollushion than generating the same amount of
electricity through water power. Still, many people portest the dissappearance of
their lands. They predict that the dam will create a dissaster.

1. _____   3. _____   5. _____

2. _____   4. _____   6. _____

Writing Activity

Write a paragraph explaining why you think the dam is a good idea or a poor one. Use
four spelling words.

_____

_____

_____

_____

Words from Social Studies

Look at the words in each set below. One word in each set is spelled correctly. Use a pencil to fill in the circle next to the correct word. Before you begin, look at the sample sets of words. Sample A has been done for you. Do Sample B by yourself. When you are sure you know what to do, you may go on with the rest of the page.

Sample A:
- (A) reacktion
- (B) re-action
- (C) reeaction
- (D) reaction ●

Sample B:
- (E) programer
- (F) programmer
- (G) programmar
- (H) programmerr

1.
(A) proceedure
(B) proscedure
(C) procedure
(D) procedsure

2.
(E) civilizacion
(F) civilization
(G) civalization
(H) civalizacion

3.
(A) replanish
(B) replenishe
(C) repplenish
(D) replenish

4.
(E) excavate
(F) excivate
(G) exscavate
(H) exscivate

5.
(A) explaination
(B) explainacion
(C) explanation
(D) explanacion

6.
(E) reknew
(F) reknoo
(G) renew
(H) renoo

7.
(A) starvation
(B) starvacion
(C) starvashun
(D) starvasion

8.
(E) exstinct
(F) extinct
(G) exctinct
(H) extinckt

9.
(A) dissprove
(B) disprouve
(C) disprove
(D) desprove

10.
(E) protektave
(F) portectave
(G) protectave
(H) protective

11.
(A) displaced
(B) dissplaced
(C) disaplaced
(D) displaiced

12.
(E) exsess
(F) exscess
(G) exess
(H) excess

13.
(A) genarations
(B) generations
(C) generacions
(D) genaracions

14.
(E) polluttion
(F) polution
(G) pollution
(H) pollucion

15.
(A) irigation
(B) irriggation
(C) irrigacion
(D) irrigation

16.
(E) prowtest
(F) protest
(G) portest
(H) prottest

17.
(A) evaporation
(B) evaperation
(C) evaporacion
(D) evaperacion

18.
(E) desaster
(F) disaster
(G) dissaster
(H) dessaster

19.
(A) revvive
(B) revyve
(C) revive
(D) reviev

20.
(E) dissappearance
(F) disappearance
(G) disapearance
(H) disappearence

Grade 6/Unit 6
A Great Wall?
20

Grade 6/Unit 6 Review Test

Read each sentence. If an underlined word is spelled wrong, fill in the circle that goes with that word. If no word is spelled wrong, fill in the circle below NONE.

Read Sample A and do Sample B.

A. Sometimes <u>jealusy</u> can <u>develop</u> in a <u>friendship</u>.
      A   B   C

NONE
A. Ⓐ Ⓑ Ⓒ Ⓓ

B. The <u>rivalry</u> <u>occurs</u> when one friend feels <u>threatened</u>.
     E   F   G

NONE
B. Ⓔ Ⓕ Ⓖ Ⓗ

1. The <u>inseperable</u> friends were <u>discontent</u> with the <u>transportation</u>.
       A   B   C

NONE
1. Ⓐ Ⓑ Ⓒ Ⓓ

2. It was <u>unecessary</u> to <u>decipher</u> the scroll from the <u>ravine</u>.
        E   F   G

NONE
2. Ⓔ Ⓕ Ⓖ Ⓗ

3. The <u>coyote</u> on the <u>sierra</u> was <u>imovable</u>.
     A   B   C

NONE
3. Ⓐ Ⓑ Ⓒ Ⓓ

4. Explain the <u>disappearance</u> of the <u>boquet</u> and <u>chandelier</u>.
           E   F   G

NONE
4. Ⓔ Ⓕ Ⓖ Ⓗ

5. We agreed to <u>postpone</u> the <u>transportation</u> of the <u>spesimens</u>.
          A   B   C

NONE
5. Ⓐ Ⓑ Ⓒ Ⓓ

6. The <u>graddual</u> <u>starvation</u> of the animals will make them <u>extinct</u>.
     E   F   G

NONE
6. Ⓔ Ⓕ Ⓖ Ⓗ

7. A child's <u>disappearance</u> will often <u>precede</u> a <u>commotion</u>.
        A   B   C

NONE
7. Ⓐ Ⓑ Ⓒ Ⓓ

8. <u>Recite</u> your <u>discantent</u> before you <u>proceed</u>.
   E   F   G

NONE
8. Ⓔ Ⓕ Ⓖ Ⓗ

9. We will <u>ekspand</u> the <u>ravine</u> to fight <u>pollution</u>.
       A   B   C

NONE
9. Ⓐ Ⓑ Ⓒ Ⓓ

10. If you <u>recite</u> the alphabet, which <u>consanant</u> will <u>precede</u>?
     E   F   G

NONE
10. Ⓔ Ⓕ Ⓖ Ⓗ

Go on

Grade 6/Unit 6 Review Test

11. It's <u>unnecesary</u> to <u>proceed</u> without the <u>specimens</u>.
    A   B   C
11. Ⓐ Ⓑ Ⓒ Ⓓ NONE

12. The animal's <u>unnecessary</u> <u>starvation</u> caused a <u>commotion</u>.
    E   F   G
12. Ⓔ Ⓕ Ⓖ Ⓗ NONE

13. It is <u>unnecessary</u> to <u>desipher</u> these <u>specimens</u>.
    A   B   C
13. Ⓐ Ⓑ Ⓒ Ⓓ NONE

14. The <u>kiyote</u> and his <u>inseparable</u> mate lived on the <u>sierra</u>.
    E   F   G
14. Ⓔ Ⓕ Ⓖ Ⓗ NONE

15. Her opinion of <u>polution</u> and <u>starvation</u> was <u>immovable</u>.
    A   B   C
15. Ⓐ Ⓑ Ⓒ Ⓓ NONE

16. The <u>bouqet</u> and its <u>disappearance</u> caused <u>discontent</u>.
    E   F   G
16. Ⓔ Ⓕ Ⓖ Ⓗ NONE

17. The <u>transsportation</u> of the <u>chandelier</u> should be <u>gradual</u>.
    A   B   C
17. Ⓐ Ⓑ Ⓒ Ⓓ NONE

18. Before we <u>proceed</u> we must <u>postpoan</u> our trip to the <u>ravine</u>.
    E   F   G
18. Ⓔ Ⓕ Ⓖ Ⓗ NONE

19. It was <u>unnecessary</u> to <u>expand</u> the <u>comotion</u>.
    A   B   C
19. Ⓐ Ⓑ Ⓒ Ⓓ NONE

20. The <u>immovable</u> <u>pollution</u> forced us to <u>replennish</u> our supply.
    E   F   G
20. Ⓔ Ⓕ Ⓖ Ⓗ NONE

21. To <u>decipher</u> the code by each <u>consonant</u> is a <u>gradual</u> process.
    A   B   C
21. Ⓐ Ⓑ Ⓒ Ⓓ NONE

22. The <u>coyote</u> may <u>expand</u> its walk in the <u>siera</u>.
    E   F   G
22. Ⓔ Ⓕ Ⓖ Ⓗ NONE

23. <u>Starrvation</u> of the animals will <u>precede</u> their <u>disappearance</u>.
    A   B   C
23. Ⓐ Ⓑ Ⓒ Ⓓ NONE

24. The <u>commotion</u> caused us to <u>postpone</u> the <u>transportation</u>.
    E   F   G
24. Ⓔ Ⓕ Ⓖ Ⓗ NONE

25. The <u>bouquet</u> is <u>unnecessary</u> unless you <u>recite</u> your vows.
    A   B   C
25. Ⓐ Ⓑ Ⓒ Ⓓ NONE